Why Psycholo

Why Psychology?

Adrian Furnham & David Oakley
University College London

First published in 1995 by UCL Press

UCL Press Limited
University College London
Gower Street
London WC1E 6BT

The name of University College London (UCL) is a registered
trade mark used by UCL Press with the consent of the owner.

ISBN: 1-85728-298-1 PB

British Library Cataloguing-in-Publication Data
A CIP catalogue record for this book is available from the British Library.

Library of Congress Cataloging-in-Publication Data are available.

Typeset in Palatino.
Printed and bound by
Page Bros (Norwich) Ltd, England.

To our students: past, present and future

Contents

Preface

Psychology is one of the most popular choices of subjects for students. This has been the case for many years but its popularity has in fact been increasing. Why is this? Psychology is a *new science*, barely one hundred years old. It is interesting and exciting experiencing a new discipline develop and change. We are understanding more and more about how the brain operates, why people behave the way they do, and the causes of human unhappiness. Any one comparing a psychology textbook written fifty years ago with a recent one will immediately see how far the science has developed and, no doubt, how much more there is to explore. Psychology is both a *pure* and an *applied science*. It aims to understand behaviour and the mechanisms and processes which make people tick. But it also tries to solve human problems and improve the human condition. In hospitals, factories, schools and in practically every human setting, psychologists have attempted to improve the quality of life by testing and applying their theories.

Psychology is *multi-disciplinary*, having close connections with many other subjects including anatomy, medicine, psychiatry and sociology as well as economics, mathematics and zoology. This means that psychology students get exposed to a wide variety of ideas, concepts and methods used in other disciplines. But psychology is also a core discipline with its own ideas and concepts. It is about *all aspects of human behaviour*. Newcomers to the subject of psychology are often surprised by the range of things that psychologists study – from dreaming to drug addiction; computer phobia to the causes of cancer; memory to social mobility; learning to lying. Psychologists tend to specialize and take a particular interest in certain psychological processes later on in their careers, but many continue to share very wide interests.

It is no wonder then that so many students express a considerable interest in, and a desire to study, psychology both later in their school careers and at university. But because few have had prior experience of psychology as an academic subject, compared to say history, mathematics or languages, many prospective students are fairly ignorant about the discipline. While psychologists are frequently asked to comment on everyday occurrences on the media, and are sometimes even portrayed in fictional stories, it is very difficult to get a balanced and informed view of what psychology is all about.

As a result many students are surprised – usually pleasantly but not always – to discover what is studied in psychology. Not all are familiar with the scope of the subject and the way it is taught. This book is an attempt to explain *what* psychology is and therefore *why* students might choose to study it. We would like you, the reader, to be an educated consumer so that you know what you are letting yourself in for. In this book we hope to dispel a few myths, correct a few erroneous beliefs and inform you about one of the most important and exciting behavioural sciences.

Why psychology? is for students in schools considering whether to take psychology alongside their more traditional subjects, for students in their later school years considering the possibility of studying psychology at college or university, for those considering a change in career, for parents, careers officers and others who advise students and prospective students of all ages, and for anyone who has ever wondered just what psychology involves but wasn't sure where to find out. Chapter 1 looks at some common ideas and misconceptions about psychology. Chapter 2 considers what psychology is (and is not), the history of psychology and the major issues it addresses. Chapter 3 discusses the methods psychologists use in investigating their subject. Chapter 4 explores what students of psychology in schools, colleges and universities might expect to be taught, and how, and looks in more detail at some typical examples of research. Chapter 5 is concerned with the way psychology is used by society and professional psychologists. Finally, Chapter 6 gives some guidance on how to take an interest in psychology further through reading or more formal study, and how that study in turn could lead to a career in psychology or other related areas.

Adrian Furnham
David Oakley
London 1994

Chapter 1
Common-sense views and misconceptions about psychology

Introduction

Is psychology more interesting and worthy of study than you might think? Students and lecturers in the subject would say so, but that is to be expected. What people who study psychology often say is that it gives you an "aha" experience. This is based on the distinction between trial-and-error learning, which involves trying out theories or hypotheses until the "correct" answer is found, and just "fiddling about" with the problem in the hope that the solution presents itself. "Aha" is the expression of surprised happiness which comes with insight.

Perhaps more importantly and usefully, psychology teaches students a rich vocabulary through which they can describe and explain behaviour. Just as going to art galleries with art historians (or even better, a tape recording of their comments) can bring paintings to life because they are able to point out and describe minor details of major significance, so psychology teaches the student the language of behavioural description. Of course there is a joke about "psychobabble", which is the mis- or overuse of psychological language and concepts, but that usually occurs only in the popular press and by non-psychologists.

There is one other great feature of psychology: a number of the theories are counterintuitive, or not what common sense suggests. It is true that some findings and theories *are* pretty commonsensical but there are also a number that are not. Indeed, it is frequently the discovery of principles and processes behind non-commonsensical findings that leads to the "aha" experience.

Nevertheless, many sceptics and some cynics have continued to maintain that all the findings in psychology really are only a form of common sense. Surely, they argue, human nature dictates what people are really like and there certainly is no shortage of opinion from philosophers on the topic of human nature.

1

Jeremy Bentham (1748–1832) described humans as rational beings, making choices and decisions in terms of enlightened self-interest. Le Bon (1841–1931) on the other hand stressed the irrationality and impulsiveness of people in crowds. Hobbes (1588–1679) viewed humans as selfish, nasty and brutish, whose striving had to be restrained by a powerful government. Rousseau (1712–78) saw the restraints of his civilization as the force that was destroying the nobility of the "natural man", the noble savage. Furthermore, there are numerous philosophical treatises which carefully compare and contrast some of the major thinkers of our time: Marx, Darwin, Freud, Lévi-Strauss, Chomsky, etc. It may also be argued that the major schools of psychology – Skinnerian behaviourism, psychoanalysis and humanistic psychology – have quite different theories about the essential nature of mankind (see Ch. 2).

Thinkers who have pondered human nature have typically asked the following sorts of questions: What are the differing views of human nature? How do these views explain behaviour in interactions among people? How do the behaviours explained and predicted by philosophies of human nature compare to the actual ongoing, observable ways in which people act? What types of societies and institutions are to be inferred from these views of human nature? How do these societies and institutions compare with existing social structures? Which of the views of human nature thus considered are most accurate? Which behaviours are most congruent and which behaviours are least congruent with this view of human nature? Where is it possible to place societal and institutional constraints upon behaviour, and how may these constraints be arranged to dampen or correct deviations and aberrations from human nature? How can constraints be placed or removed in order to maximize the good in man's basic nature?

The psychologist Wrightsman (1964) has argued that people's beliefs about human nature differ along six basic dimensions, each with positive and negative poles, which form the basis for his Philosophy of Human Nature Scale. The six dimensions are as follows:

1. *Trustworthiness vs untrustworthiness*
   + = belief that people are trustworthy, moral and responsible
   − = belief that people are untrustworthy, immoral and irresponsible
2. *Strength of will and rationality vs lack of willpower and irrationality*
   + = belief that people can control their outcomes and that they understand themselves
   − = belief that people lack self-determination and are irrational
3. *Altruism vs selfishness*
   + = belief that people are altruistic, unselfish and sincerely interested in others
   − = belief that people are selfish and self-centred

4. *Independence vs conformity to group pressures*
    + = belief that people are able to maintain their beliefs in the face of group pressures to the contrary
    − = belief that people give in to pressures of group and society
5. *Variability vs similarity*
    + = belief that people are different from each other in personality and interests and that a person can change over time
    − = belief that people are similar in interests and are not changeable over time
6. *Complexity vs simplicity*
    + = belief that people are complex and hard to understand
    − = belief that people are simple and easy to understand

Two of these dimensions of human nature concern beliefs in the variation that exists among individuals: similarity vs variability and complexity vs simplicity. So Wrightsman's six-dimension scale can be divided into two major variables or subscales: *positive–negative* (incorporating the dimensions of strength of will, trust, independence and altruism) and *multiplexity* (covering variability and complexity) which are by and large independent of one another.

One way to discover the real nature of human nature is, according to most psychologists, scientific experimentation and observation, but lay people do not use scientific evidence when forming their ideas about their fellows. Many believe in superstitions and old-wives' tales that have been perpetuated, but never tested, over the generations.

Superstition versus science

There has been a long-standing interest in the knowledge, beliefs and superstitions (or "unsubstantiated beliefs") that students bring to social science courses. In 1925 Nixon sought to demonstrate that his students arrived at the beginning of his psychology classes with a variety of unsubstantiated beliefs about human behaviour, but that these changed as a function of teaching. He gave over 350 students a 30-item *true–false* test containing items such as "Many eminent men have been feeble-minded as children", "A square jaw is a sign of will-power" and "The marriage of cousins is practically certain to result in children of inferior intelligence". Over half of this sample believed: "Intelligence can be increased with training", "The study of mathematics is valuable because it gives one a logical mind", "Man is superior because his conduct is very largely guided by reason", "Adults sometimes become feeble-minded from over-study" and "You can estimate an individual's intelligence pretty closely by just looking at his face".

Twenty-five years later Levitt (1952) replicated this study on superstition. He defined superstition as a belief which is irrational; popularly accepted; usually influences the behaviour of the holder; may relate to supernatural phenomena; has no sound evidence of personal experience to support it and arises spontaneously and spreads without ever having had the sanction of authority. The same questionnaire was administered to 100 men and the results compared with those of Nixon. Overall, there was a significant decline in superstitious beliefs. Some superstitions, like those concerning phrenology and physiognomy (determining a person's character by examining bumps on their skull or from the appearance of their face), he believed had become extinct, though he noted that others which had declined, such as those concerning magic, would probably find modern replacements. The author concluded that superstitions (or cognitive distortions) must be important to the individual (otherwise they would not be held), ambiguous (because the true facts are lacking or concealed) and related to certain personality factors (insecure, anxious, neurotically prone).

Over thirty years later Tupper and Williams (1986) replicated the study in Australia and found the level of superstition back up to 21 per cent compared to Nixon (1925) at 30.4 per cent and Levitt (1952) at 6.5 per cent. Thus, instead of seeing a steady decline in superstitious beliefs over time, the results are moderately consistent between 1925 and 1986. These results do show a modest decline but not as much as predicted by Nixon and indeed an increase on Levitt. Of course, it may well be that methodological artefacts account for these results: for example, Levitt only had male subjects; Tupper and Williams' (1986) study was done in Australia; and subjects from all three groups were not comparable in terms of education. On the other hand, it may well be that superstitious, non-scientific beliefs regarding human nature have only marginally decreased over time. Many researchers believe that although these superstitious beliefs may be culturally relative and changeable following fashions, they are unlikely to decline greatly as they fulfil an important psychological function, namely the reduction of anxiety.

Gregory (1975) replicated a study by Conklin (1919) on genuine superstitions in college students, such as a belief in lucky symbols (black cats, the number 13, broken mirrors). The results showed that superstitious beliefs and practices had changed rather than declined over time. For instance, carrying lucky rabbits' feet or avoiding pavement (sidewalk) cracks were no longer held important, while saving certain coins and finding horse shoes were thought to be even more lucky than was thought in the past.

But how superstitious are you? Nearly fifty years ago an American psychologist called Ralya gave the following test to medical students. Read each question and decide if it is true or false.

Test 1 *Beliefs about human nature**

1. The position of the stars at the time of a man's birth determines, in part, his character. TRUE/FALSE
2. The ancient Greeks were born with better intellects than people are endowed with today. TRUE/FALSE
3. Man is biologically descended from a species of existing apes. TRUE/FALSE
4. Apes have been known to solve problems that the average three-year-old child could not solve. TRUE/FALSE
5. Some of the higher apes are as intelligent as the average man. TRUE/FALSE
6. Animals depend to a greater extent on inherited ways of doing things than does man. TRUE/FALSE
7. The conscience is part of man's natural equipment at birth. TRUE/FALSE
8. Mothers instinctively know the best ways of caring for their children. TRUE/FALSE
9. Most children are born bad. TRUE/FALSE
10. Most children are born good. TRUE/FALSE
11. Human nature cannot be changed since it is based upon instincts. TRUE/FALSE
12. All people reach physical maturity by the age of eighteen. TRUE/FALSE
14. All traits present in a child at birth are inherited traits. TRUE/FALSE
15. All traits appearing in a child after birth are the results of environmental influence. TRUE/FALSE
16. With the exception of identical twins, it is extremely unlikely that any two people have exactly the same heredity. TRUE/FALSE
17. Voodooism is in the blood of the negro. TRUE/FALSE
18. An English-speaking person with German ancestors finds it easier to learn German than an English-speaking person with French ancestors. TRUE/FALSE
19. If the tails are cut off of generation after generation of rats, eventually rats without tails will be born. TRUE/FALSE
20. An average child of the caveman of 10,000 years ago, if brought up in an American home of today, would in all probability become an ordinary American adult. TRUE/FALSE
21. Human progress is due to increased native intelligence from age to age. TRUE/FALSE
22. All men are born with equal powers. TRUE/FALSE
23. The average white man is born superior, intellectually, to the average man of any other race. TRUE/FALSE
24. Primitive people are born with keener senses than the more highly civilized. TRUE/FALSE

25. On average, men are born superior, intellectually, to women. TRUE/FALSE
26. People cannot be sharply differentiated into blondes and brunettes in many cases. TRUE/FALSE
27. If we knew all about a person's heredity we could predict his success in the world. TRUE/FALSE
28. Any child, if carefully trained from birth could be made into a successful doctor, lawyer, engineer or journalist. TRUE/FALSE
29. Geniuses are always successful, whatever the handicaps of their environment. TRUE/FALSE
30. Most great men have been born of poor but honest parents. TRUE/FALSE
31. On average, the strongest men physically are the weakest mentally. TRUE/FALSE
32. Homely women are born with more intelligence than beautiful women. TRUE/FALSE
33. Brilliant children are more subject to brain fever than children of average or subnormal intelligence. TRUE/FALSE
34. No defect of body or mind can hold us back if we have will-power enough. TRUE/FALSE
35. Faith alone can heal a broken leg. TRUE/FALSE
36. Intelligence plays a larger role in human happiness than does emotion. TRUE/FALSE
37. We are more likely to become fatigued from work that does not interest us than from work that does interest us. TRUE/FALSE
38. A person who is fatigued invariably does poorer work than the same person fully rested. TRUE/FALSE
39. Two individuals of the same intelligence will give almost identical testimony concerning an accident which they have both witnessed. TRUE/FALSE
40. All of man's actions are determined by his desire to seek pleasure and avoid pain. TRUE/FALSE
41. A man's character can be read by noting the size and location of certain developments on his head. TRUE/FALSE
42. Certain lines on a person's hand are indicative of his future. TRUE/FALSE
43. People with long fingers are likely to be artistic. TRUE/FALSE
45. Red-headed people are likely to be temperamental. TRUE/FALSE
46. Large-mouthed people are likely to be generous. TRUE/FALSE
47. Green-eyed people are likely to be more jealous than blue-eyed people. TRUE/FALSE
48. Brunettes are more trustworthy than blondes. TRUE/FALSE
49. Cold hands are a sign of a warm heart. TRUE/FALSE
50. A person who holds his thumbs in his hands is a coward. TRUE/FALSE

51. A person may be a coward in one situation and not in another. TRUE/FALSE
52. Illegible handwriting is a sign of superior intelligence in the educated adults. TRUE/FALSE
53. If your ears burn it is a sign that someone is talking about you. TRUE/FALSE
54. It is unlucky to have anything to do with the number 13. TRUE/FALSE
55. Beginning an undertaking on Friday is almost sure to bring bad luck. TRUE/FALSE

* Nos 13 and 44 were missing from the original test.

Items 4, 6, 16, 20, 26, 37 and 51 are probably true, the rest are false. If you got more than 48 correct, well done. Most people score between 30 and 35, which shows they remain relatively ignorant about much of psychology; worse, they are superstitious or racist!

Common sense

To many people, the theories they come across in a number of the social sciences – psychology, management, sociology, criminology – are common sense. That is, the theories of findings are already well known, and hence the research is thought to be a trivial, expensive and pointless exercise describing or providing what we already know. Being sensitive to this criticism, which is naturally seen as misplaced, social scientists have often confronted this point at the beginning of their textbooks,

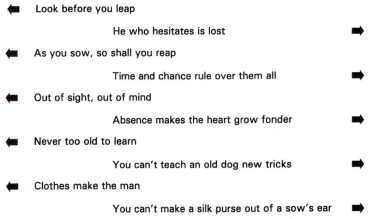

Figure 1.1 The Trouble with Folk Wisdom is that it Gives No Guide for Determining Which of the Two Contradictory Sayings is Appropriate in a Particular Situation. Thus the Usefulness of Such Sayings is Quite Limited. Reprinted with permission from W. McKeachie & C. Doyle, *Psychology* (Reading, Mass.: Addison-Wesley, 1966).

warning readers of the dangers of common sense which lulls people into the false belief that they understand others. Some have even provocatively mentioned the term "uncommon sense" in their writing.

For instance, McKeachie and Doyle (1966) begin their general psychology textbook asking how a scientific explanation is different from common sense, and present Figure 1.1.

Why not test yourself? Below are 40 statements that you must decide are either true or false. See how much common sense helps you to give the correct answer.

Test 2 *Common sense*

1. In general, women conform more than men.   TRUE/FALSE
2. In bargaining with others, it is best to start with a moderate offer – one close to the final agreement desired.   TRUE/FALSE
3. In making decisions, committees tend to be more conservative than individuals.   TRUE/FALSE
4. Dangerous riots are most likely to occur when temperatures reach extremely high levels (e.g. around 95–100°F).   TRUE/FALSE
5. The more persons present at the scene of an emergency, the more likely the victims are to receive help.   TRUE/FALSE
6. If you pay someone for doing something they enjoy, they will come to like this task even more.   TRUE/FALSE
7. In choosing their romantic partners, most people show a strong preference for extremely attractive persons.   TRUE/FALSE
8. If you want to get someone to change his or her views, it is best to offer this person a very large reward for doing so.   TRUE/FALSE
9. When a stranger stands very close to us, we usually interpret this as a sign of friendliness and react in a positive manner.   TRUE/FALSE
10. Most people feel sympathy for the victims of serious accidents or natural disasters and do not hold such persons responsible for the harm they have suffered.   TRUE/FALSE
11. Unpleasant environmental conditions (e.g. crowding, loud noise, high temperatures) produce immediate reductions in performance on many tasks.   TRUE/FALSE
12. Directive, authoritative leaders are generally best in attaining high levels of productivity from their subordinates.   TRUE/FALSE
13. In most cases, individuals act in ways that are consistent with their attitudes about various issues.   TRUE/FALSE
14. Top executives are usually extremely competitive, hard-driving types.   TRUE/FALSE
15. Most persons are much more concerned with the size of their own salary than with the salary of others.   TRUE/FALSE

16. Direct, face-to-face communication usually enhances co-operation between individuals. TRUE/FALSE

17. Most persons prefer challenging jobs with a great deal of freedom and autonomy. TRUE/FALSE

18. The behaviour of most lower animals – insects, reptiles and amphibians, most rodents and birds – is instinctive and unaffected by learning. TRUE/FALSE

19. For the first week of its life, a baby sees nothing but a grey blue regardless of what he or she "looks at". TRUE/FALSE

20. A child learns to talk more quickly if the adult around it habitually repeats the word it is trying to say, using proper pronunciation. TRUE/FALSE

21. The best way to get a chronically noisy schoolchild to settle down and pay attention is to punish it. TRUE/FALSE

22. Slow learners remember more of what they learn than fast learners. TRUE/FALSE

23. Highly intelligent people – "geniuses" – tend to be physically frail and socially isolated. TRUE/FALSE

24. On average, you cannot predict from a person's grades at school and college whether he or she will do well in a career. TRUE/FALSE

25. Most national and ethnic stereotypes are completely false. TRUE/FALSE

26. In small amounts alcohol is a stimulant. TRUE/FALSE

27. LSD causes chromosome damage. TRUE/FALSE

28. The largest drug problem in Britain, in terms of the number of people affected, is marijuana. TRUE/FALSE

29. Psychiatry is a subdivision of psychology. TRUE/FALSE

30. Most mentally retarded people are also mentally ill. TRUE/FALSE

31. Electroshock therapy is an outmoded technique rarely used in today's mental hospitals. TRUE/FALSE

32. The more severe the disorder, the more intensive the therapy required to cure it, for example, schizophrenics usually respond best to psychoanalysis. TRUE/FALSE

33. Quite a few psychological characteristics of men and women appear to be inborn in all cultures, for example, women are more emotional and sexually less aggressive than men. TRUE/FALSE

34. No reputable psychologist "believes in" such irrational phenomena as ESP, hypnosis, or the bizarre mental and physical achievements of Eastern yogis. TRUE/FALSE

35. To change people's behaviour towards members of ethnic minority groups, we must first change their attitudes. TRUE/FALSE

36. The basis of the baby's love for its mother is the fact that its mother fills its physiological needs for food, etc. TRUE/FALSE

37. The more highly motivated you are, the better you will do at solving complex problems.   TRUE/FALSE
38. The best way to ensure that a desired behaviour will persist after training is completed is to reward the behaviour every single time it occurs throughout training (rather than intermittently).   TRUE/FALSE
39. A schizophrenic is someone with a split personality.   TRUE/FALSE
40. The best way to stop a malicious rumour at work is to present contrary evidence against it.   TRUE/FALSE.

Total up the FALSE-score, because the statements are *all* false for different reasons which have been discovered by psychological experiments or observations. How did *you* score? Do *you* think psychology is just common sense? Why then do people keep making this objection? Essentially one can make three points. The first – that the findings are well known, intuitive, unsurprising, uninformative, etc. – has been discussed. The second is that psychological accounts of issues which are the "stuff of personal experience" (person perception, job motivation, love and attraction) have tended – either by use of excessive jargon or technical language, or the focusing on minute, esoteric, trivial or irrelevant aspects of social behaviour – to debase or corrupt common sense. That is, topics that are amenable to common sense should have explanations in terms of common sense.

A third, related, objection occurs when experimental findings or social science writings appear to contradict widely held views of human nature. Nearly all social psychological findings which have demonstrated that people are cruel, uninsightful, self-centred, compliant, anti-social have been criticized more than those findings that have painted the opposite picture. That is, objections are made where findings are against the consensus, or common-sense, view that people are basically good, altruistic and intelligent.

Some people believe that *all* of science is common sense. Paradoxically, it is the "hard" scientists who are most convinced that all science is just common sense. Huxley (1902), a famous British scientist, noted:

> Science is nothing but trained and organized Common Sense, differing from the latter only as a veteran may differ from a raw recruit: and its methods differ from those of Common Sense only as far as the guardsman's cut and thrust differ from the manner in which a savage wields his club . . . (p. 42)

Whitehead, another well-known scientist, is reputed to have said that "Science is rooted in the whole apparatus of Common Sense thought". Other scientists have dismissed common sense as a source of ideas, let alone testable theories: some psychologists have been particularly dismissive of the importance of common sense. Skinner (1972) wrote:

"What, after all, have we to show for non-scientific or prescientific good judgement, or common sense, or the insights gained through personal experience? It is science of nothing" (p. 160). Eysenck (1957) in his celebrated book *Sense and nonsense in psychology* states:

> This is only one example of what appears to be an almost universal belief to the effect that anyone is competent to discuss psychological problems, whether he has taken the trouble to study the subject or not and that while everybody's opinion is of equal value, that of the professional psychologist must be excluded at all costs because he might spoil the fun by producing some facts which would completely upset the speculation and the wonderful dream castles so laboriously constructed by the layman. (p. 3)

Thus for these eminent psychologists common sense is a dangerous area from which to draw ideas, as lay beliefs are often misguided or untestable. Even worse, various "common-sense" ideas may be based not on simple surmise but prejudice and political ideology. Moreover, one can cite extensive literature that illustrates lay persons' "faulty" reasoning, e.g. the readily observed failure of lay people to make appropriate use of disconfirmatory information in problem solving and the overwhelming preference for confirmatory strategies in logical reasoning tasks. For example, if you want to find out if somebody is an extrovert you can ask whether he or she has many friends, likes going out, and really enjoys parties (confirmatory) or, alternatively, whether they are rather shy in company (disconfirmatory). Lay people prefer to use the first of these two approaches and to ignore any disconfirmatory information which might be available.

There are many other well-established findings showing human irrationality in everyday settings. For example, people overestimate the frequency of well-publicized events (deaths attributable to being murdered or having cancer) while underestimating less-publicized events (like dying from asthma or diabetes). Similarly, when considering say the relative job performance of two people, the absolute number of successes is given greater weight than the relative number of successes to failures – people ignore the denominator. There are many, many examples of this type of faulty reasoning.

So the argument ebbs and flows. Is psychology a science? Is science a good thing? Is science common sense? Consider the quotes in Table 1.1.

It should be clear that there is no agreement on this issue! It could be argued that psychology is, in part, the scientific study of common sense.

Table 1.1 A battery of quotes for and against science and common sense.

Pro-science

A scientist is a man who would rather count than guess. *M. Gluckman*

Science is organized common sense where many a beautiful theory is filled by an ugly fact. *T. H. Huxley*

Science may be described as the art of systematic oversimplification. *K. Popper*

The man of science does not discover in order to know: he wants to know in order to discover. *A. N. Whitehead*

Science increases our power in proportion as it lowers our pride. *C. Bernard*

Science is what you know, philosophy is what you don't know. *B. Russell*

You know very well that unless you are a scientist, it's much more important for a theory to be shapely, than for it to be true. *C. Hampton*

Anti-science

Science is always wrong: it never solves a problem without creating ten more. *G. B. Shaw*

I am tired of all this thing called science . . . We have spent millions on that sort of thing for the last few years, and it is time it should be stopped. *S. Cameron*

One of the most pernicious falsehoods ever to be universally accepted is that scientific method is the only reliable way to truth. *R. Bube*

Traditional scientific method has always been, at the very least, 20–20 hindsight. It's good for seeing where you've been. *R. Pirsig*

Though many have tried, no-one has ever yet explained away the decisive fact that science, which can do so much, cannot decide what it ought to do. *J. W. Krutch*

Look at those cows and remember that the greater scientists in the world have not discovered how to make grass into milk. *M. Pulin*

Pro-common sense

It is a thousand times better to have common sense without education than to have education without common sense. *R. Ingersol*

Common sense in an uncommon degree is what the world calls wisdom. *S. T. Coleridge.*

The philosophy of one century is the common sense of the next. *H. W. Beecher*

The best prophet is common sense. *Euripides*

If a man has common sense he has all the sense there is. *S. Rayburn*

Common sense is instinct and enough of it is genius. *H. W. Shaw*

Common sense is the wick of the candle. *R. W. Emerson*

Fine sense and exalted sense are not half so useful as common sense. *B. Gracian*

The crown of all faculties is common sense. It is not enough to do the right thing: it must be done at the right time, and place. *W. Matthews*

Anti-common sense

Common sense is the collection of prejudices people have accrued by the age of 18. *A. Einstein*

Logic is one thing and common sense another. *E. Hubbard*

Anti-common sense (continued)

Common sense is in spite of, not the result of, education. *V. Hugo*

Common sense is, of all kinds, the most uncommon. *T. Edwards*

Common sense, however logical and sound, is after all only one human attitude among many others, and like everything human, it may have its limitations – or negative side. *W. Barrett*

Common sense is the most fairly distributed thing in the world, for each thinks he is so well endowed with it that even those who are hardest to satisfy in all other matters are not in the habit of desiring more of it than they already have. *R. Descartes*

If common sense were as unerring as calculus, as some suggest, I don't understand why so many mistakes are made so often by so many people. *C. Winkel*

Knowledge about psychology

We have looked at superstition and common sense. Finally, we shall look at your psychological knowledge. This is a multiple-choice test that asks you to guess the correct answer – out of 4 – and also to say how much interest you have in the topic. Have a go.

Test 3 *Knowledge about psychology*

The following quiz allows you to demonstrate what you know about psychology. The items have been selected to represent a wide variety of topics and to reflect public interest in psychological issues. For each item one choice is clearly better than the other three, as determined by examining the relevant scientific evidence. The test is not timed, but try not to linger very long on an item.

We would also like to know your interest in the topic addressed by each item. Below each item you will find the question "How interesting to you is the topic of this item?", followed by a blank. We would like you to use this scale to answer each of these questions: 1 = very uninteresting; 2 = uninteresting; 3 = I am indifferent; 4 = interesting; 5 = very interesting.

For example, one of the quiz items is concerned with the psychological effects of a full moon. Regardless of how you answered this item we want to know how personally interesting the topic of "the psychological effects of a full moon" is to you. If you are very interested in learning more about it, put a "5" in the blank. If you think the topic is very boring then put a "1" in the blank.

1. Over the last twenty years the total number of deaths or severe injuries in the USA caused by "maniacs" who put razor blades or poison in Halloween pumpkins is ____.

   a. 0–25
   b. 26–50

    c. 51–500

    d. more than 500

    How interesting to you is the topic of this item ? ____

2. Most of the research supports the conclusion that ____ are more likely to occur when the moon is full.

    a. traffic accidents

    b. homicides

    c. both of the above

    d. neither of the above

    How interesting to you is the topic of this item? ____

3. Regular marijuana usage eventually causes people to use ____.

    a. cocaine

    b. heroin

    c. both of the above

    d. neither of the above

    How interesting to you is the topic of this item? ____

4. Some of the learning principles which apply to birds and fish also apply to ____.

    a. cockroaches

    b. humans

    c. both of the above

    d. neither of the above

    How interesting to you is the topic of this item? ____

5. Consider the old saying "Beauty is only skin deep." Generally speaking, research shows that physically attractive people are ____ physically unattractive persons.

    a. likely to be more psychologically stable than

    b. equal in psychological stability to

    c. likely to be less psychologically stable than

    d. likely to be far less psychologically stable than

    How interesting to you is the topic of this item? ____

6. Generally speaking the saying, "Opposites attract" is ____ description of how people come to like one another.

    a. an almost true

    b. a very accurate

    c. a somewhat accurate

    d. usually an inaccurate

    How interesting to you is the topic of this item? ____

7. Eyewitnesses to crime often give testimony in court that is ____.

    a. very inaccurate

    b. very accurate

    c. irrelevant

    d. deliberately false

    How interesting to you is the topic of this item? ____

8. The polygraph lie detector test, as a measure of whether someone

is lying or telling the truth, is accurate ____.
a. 91–100% of the time
b. 75–90% of the time
c. 55–74% of the time
d. 54% of the time or worse
How interesting to you is the topic of this item? ____

9. The earliest that human beings are capable of learning is ____.
   a. when they are still in the womb. At that time learning ability is already highly developed. For example, playing the piano a lot during pregnancy will eventually cause the child to learn to play the piano more easily.
   b. when they are still in the womb. At that time learning ability is very limited. Foetuses are capable of learning only very simple tasks.
   c. at birth. At that time learning ability is already highly developed. For example, playing the piano a lot for several months immediately following the birth of a child will eventually cause the child to learn to play the piano more easily.
   d. at birth. At that time learning ability is very limited. Newborns are capable of learning only very simple tasks.
   How interesting to you is the topic of this item? ____

10. Which of these statements about the value of teenage employment is/are true?
    a. Jobs help teenagers learn the value of money
    b. Having a job teaches teenagers to respect work
    c. neither of the above
    d. both of the above
    How interesting to you is the topic of this item? ____

11. Sigmund Freud's psychoanalytic theory is an excellent example of ____.
    a. what a well-constructed scientific theory should be like.
    b. a theory that is accepted today by almost all American/British psychologists
    c. both of the above
    d. neither of the above
    How interesting to you is the topic of this item? ____

12. Several bartenders and policemen had a chance to observe (one at a time) several target persons walk and talk for a few minutes. These target persons were either legally drunk (in most states) or sober, or they were pretending to be either drunk or sober. Which group was accurate in determining whether the target persons were *actually* drunk?
    a. most of the bartenders
    b. most of the policemen
    c. both of the above

    d. neither of the above

How interesting to you is the topic of this item? ____

13. Results on the effects of pornography depicting consenting adults show that it causes ____.
    a. an increase in aggression
    b. an increase in sex crimes
    c. neither
    d. both

How interesting to you is the topic of this item? ____

14. Research suggests that if you know someone's attitude about x you can predict behaviour relevant to x with ____.
    a. 100% accuracy
    b. 80% accuracy
    c. a small amount of accuracy
    d. no accuracy whatsoever

How interesting to you is the topic of this item? ____

15. Which of these statements is/are true?
    a. Education can be improved by opening more private schools
    b. Student achievement in private schools exceeds that in public schools
    c. both of the above
    d. neither of the above

How interesting to you is the topic of this item? ____

16. In normal human beings the ____.
    a. two hemispheres of the brain work independently
    b. "right-brained" are more creative than the "left-brained"
    c. neither of the above
    d. both of the above

How interesting to you is the topic of this item? ____

17. The percentage of child-abusing parents who are neither psychotic, mentally retarded, nor brain-damaged is approximately ____.
    a. 90%
    b. 65%
    c. 40%
    d. 15%

How interesting to you is the topic of this item? ____

18. From a psychological standpoint the most accurate statement about feeding infants is ____
    a. breast is best
    b. bottle-fed infants develop the most pleasant personalities.
    c. cup-fed infants become unusually well-adjusted adults.
    d. that the three methods are about equal

How interesting to you is the topic of this item? ____

19. On a four-choice multiple-choice test, such as this one, if you

decided to change an answer the most likely consequence is ____.
a. a change from the right answer to a wrong one
b. a change from one wrong answer to another wrong one
c. a change from a wrong answer to the right one
d. that all three possibilities are about equally likely
How interesting to you is the topic of this item? ____

20. Alcohol consumption in small doses causes people to become ____.
a. more aggressive
b. sexually aroused
c. both of the above
d. neither of the above
How interesting to you is the topic of this item? ____

21. Testosterone is a hormone that is important for human male sexual behaviour. If you were to increase greatly the amount of it in the bloodstream of a normal, healthy young man, the most likely result would be ____.
a. a large increase in sexual behaviour
b. a moderate increase in sexual behaviour
c. little or no increase in sexual behaviour
d. a decrease in sexual behaviour
How interesting to you is the topic of this item? ____

22. Under hypnosis a person will, if asked by the hypnotist, ____.
a. recall childhood events with very high accuracy
b. be able to perform physical feats of strength that would otherwise be impossible.
c. both of the above
d. neither of the above
How interesting to you is the topic of this item? ____

23. Psychologists have been accused of torturing laboratory animals. Objective studies designed to investigate these claims have found that animals are ____.
a. never subjected to any pain or harm
b. killed or badly injured in about 40% of all experiments
c. rarely killed or caused much suffering during an experiment
d. given electric shocks in about 35% of all experiments
How interesting to you is the topic of this item? ____

24. Approximately ____ per cent of all American psychologists are primarily psychotherapists. In other words, they try to help patients who have psychological problems.
a. 95
b. 75
c. 55
d. 40
How interesting to you is the topic of this item? ____

25. IQ tests given to 10-year-old children usually provide moderately accurate predictions about how ____.
    a. well adjusted you will be as an adult
    b. well you will do academically in high school
    c. many and which people should be hired for an easy job
    d. none of the above
    How interesting to you is the topic of this item? ____

26. Which of these groups is likely to be more violent as determined by several measures of violence?
    a. those with less than a high-school education
    b. high-school graduates
    c. college graduates
    d. there is very little difference among the three
    How interesting to you is the topic of this item? ____

27. Having a dry mouth is ____ why people drink fluids.
    a. the single most important reason
    b. one of the most important reasons
    c. a moderately important reason
    d. a relatively unimportant reason
    How interesting to you is the topic of this item? ____

28. Schizophrenic patients are ____.
    a. usually not dangerous to others
    b. moderately dangerous to others
    c. very dangerous to others
    d. dangerous only when their personalities "split"
    How interesting to you is the topic of this item? ____

29. Research generally supports the idea that criminals are more likely than non-criminals to ____.
    a. be ugly
    b. be obese
    c. both of the above
    d. neither of the above
    How interesting to you is the topic of this item? ____

30. The Rorschach Method, in which subjects tell what they "see" in several inkblots, is one of the most famous of all psychological tests. Which of these statements is/are accurate?
    a. Many testing experts feel that it is virtually worthless
    b. The instruction for giving the Rorschach are always given the same way to each subject
    c. both of the above
    d. neither of the above
    How interesting to you is the topic of this item? ____

31. A persuasive message is flashed on a screen so quickly that you can't see it, or whispered on an audio tape so softly that you can't hear it (subliminal perception). Which of the following statements

about subliminal perception is most accurate?
a. Studies show that subliminal perception is impossible
b. The effect is powerful enough to cause people to buy expensive items they don't want
c. It had produced weak effects in the laboratory
d. It is so influential that it can cause honest people to commit crimes

How interesting to you is the topic of this item? ____

32. In main judgements about the amount of control they have in a situation, or judgements about their own social skills the most accurate estimates are likely to be made by ____.
a. depressed patients
b. psychotic patients
c. normal people
d. people suffering from asthma

How interesting to you is the topic of this item? ____

33. Biorhythm theory holds that there are three monthly cycles: emotional, intellectual and physical. This theory has been found to be ____ in predicting injuries and the quality of human performance.
a. very successful except for the intellectual cycle
b. very successful
c. moderately successful
d. mostly unsuccessful

How interesting to you is the topic of this item? ____

34. Many hospitals encourage immediate contact between parents and newborns for several minutes right after birth because this is thought to be necessary for "bonding" to occur. Evidence that this procedure causes close relationships to develop ("bonding") between parents and child is ____.
a. very strong
b. moderately strong
c. strong only in Mormon and Catholic families
d. weak

How interesting to you is the topic of this item? ____

35. The "only" child usually turns out to be ____.
a. "spoiled"
b. about average in psychological adjustment
c. less intelligent than children who have 3 or more siblings
d. lonely

How interesting to you is the topic of this item? ____

36. People who typically spend nine or more hours sleeping at night tend to be ____ as compared with those who sleep six hours or less.
a. more concerned about personal achievement
b. a little more lazy

    c. a lot more lazy

    d. less anxious

    How interesting to you is the topic of this item? ____

37. After training has been completed, the best way to make sure that a desired behaviour will continue at a high rate is to ____.

    a. reward it every time it occurs

    b. reward it occasionally and irregularly

    c. reward it regularly once out of ever 50 times it occurs

    d. use mild punishment when the behaviour does *not* occur

    How interesting to you is the topic of this item? ____

38. When natural disasters such as hurricanes and floods strike, which of these is a common response?

    a. A large percentage of the people flee an approaching disaster

    b. Most people panic and lose their capacity to make good decisions

    c. neither of the above

    d. both of the above

    How interesting to you is the topic of this item? ____

39. Generally speaking, young geniuses (those with very high IQ scores) are found to ____.

    a. be somewhat weaker physically than normal children

    b. "burn out" quickly. As adults they lead average lives

    c. both of the above

    d. neither of the above

    How interesting to you is the topic of this item? ____

40. One electric shock of low intensity, delivered directly to the cortex of the human brain, is most likely to result in ____.

    a. pain, but no tissue destruction

    b. pain, and much tissue destruction

    c. much tissue destruction, but little pain

    d. none of the above

    How interesting to you is the topic of this item? ____

41. As a predictor of personality, handwriting analysis is generally ____.

    a. worthless

    b. slightly better than worthless

    c. fairly accurate

    d. very accurate

    How interesting to you is the topic of this item? ____

42. People who participate in dangerous sports like auto racing or sky diving are ____.

    a. better adjusted psychologically than the average person

    b. about average in adjustment

    c. about average except for a strong death wish

    d. severely disturbed

How interesting to you is the topic of this item ——

43. Astrology ____ as a predictor of human personality.
    a. has no accuracy
    b. has a small degree of accuracy
    c. is moderately accurate
    d. is very accurate
    How interesting to you is the topic of this item? ____

44. Which statement best describes the relationship between sleep and learning?
    a. It is possible to learn efficiently while you are in deep sleep
    b. Learning is efficient when it is followed by sleep
    c. It is a great idea to sleep, then study immediately upon awakening
    d. Sleep is totally unrelated to learning efficiency
    How interesting to you is the topic of this item? ____

45. Does research on sleep show that (1) sleepwalkers are acting out their dreams and (2) sleeptalkers often give away their secrets during sleep?
    a. Number one is true but number two is not
    b. Number two is true but number one is not
    c. Both are false
    d. Both are true
    How interesting to you is the topic of this item? ____

46. Which of these statements about suicide is/are true?
    a. Those who threaten to commit suicide are serious
    b. Questioning persons about their suicidal ideas may "put the idea in their head", making an attempt likely
    c. both of the above
    d. neither of the above
    How interesting to you is the topic of this item? ____

47. Many experts believe that adult humans with no brain damage use ____ of their brain cells.
    a. most
    b. about 25%
    c. about 10%
    d. less than 5%
    How interesting to you is the topic of this item? ____

48. Most reading difficulties in children are caused by ____.
    a. dyslexia
    b. the brain's reversal of words (e.g. "saw" instead of "was")
    c. neither of the above
    d. both of the above
    How interesting to you is the topic of this item? ____

49. A psychic is one who can predict the future without the use of past events. When tested under controlled laboratory conditions

psychics usually show success rates that are about ____ percentage points above chance levels.
a. 5
b. 25
c. 45
d. 65
How interesting to you is the topic of this item? ____

50. Every year during the Christmas season the ____.
a. number of admissions to mental hospitals rises rapidly
b. frequency of suicide increases
c. both of the above
d. neither of the above
How interesting to you is the topic of this item? ____

51. In 1973 it was proposed that hyperactivity in children could be successfully treated by reducing the intake of food additives (Feingold diet). Most of the evidence gathered to test this hypothesis has found that ____.
a. hyperactive children actually become more hyperactive
b. the diet has little or no effect on hyperactivity
c. hyperactive children show moderate improvement
d. the diet results in a large reduction in hyperactivity
How interesting to you is the topic of this item? ____

52. Blind people are able to avoid obstacles because they ____.
a. have a special sense which compensates for their absence of vision
b. have a greater ability to hear than sighted persons
c. both of the above
d. neither of the above
How interesting to you is the topic of this item? ____

53. The term "blue Monday" means that people are more likely to feel "blue" (sad, in a bad mood, depressed) on Monday than any other day of the week. Evidence suggests that Monday is about ____.
a. 30% "bluer" than the other days
b. 20% "bluer" than the other weekdays
c. as "blue" as other weekdays
d. as happy as Saturday and Sunday
How interesting to you is the topic of this item? ____

54. It has been claimed that some rock and roll songs, when played backwards, contain messages that promote illegal drug use and immoral behaviour (backmasking). It is further claimed that these messages cause people to behave illegally and immorally. Research on backmasking suggests that it has ____ effect on behaviour.
a. a strong negative
b. a weak negative

c. no negative
d. a weak positive
How interesting to you is the topic of this item? ____

55. When rioters are compared with non-rioters from the same community, which of these kinds of people are likely to be over-represented in groups of rioters?
    a. poorly educated
    b. those who suffer from a variety of psychological disorders
    c. neither of the above
    d. both of the above
    How interesting to you is the topic of this item? ____

56. Generally speaking, the most accurate description of the relationship between neatness and work productivity is ____.
    a. productivity is much higher in neat settings
    b. productivity is a little bit higher in neat settings
    c. productivity is the same in neat and messy settings
    d. productivity is a little bit higher in messy settings
    How interesting to you is the topic of this item? ____

57. The statement "In order to change someone's behaviour permanently you must first change that person's attitude" has been found to be ____.
    a. false, if the person can be persuaded to change behaviour for a large sum of money
    b. false, if the person can be persuaded to change behaviour for a small sum of money
    c. false, if the person is forced to change his/her behaviour
    d. true
    How interesting to you is the topic of this item? ____

58. It has been documented that some mentally retarded persons have remarkable achievements in one area. For example, some otherwise retarded persons can add huge sums of numbers quickly and accurately, while others are very musically talented. How common is this?
    a. Nearly all retarded persons have one remarkable skill
    b. About half do
    c. About one-fourth do
    d. Very few do
    How interesting to you is the topic of this item? ____

59. There are many different programmes designed to help people who want to give up cigarette smoking. In the long run (6–12 months after the programme is over), the average amount of smoking reduction is ____.
    a. about 35–50%
    b. less than it is for those who try to quit on their own
    c. both of the above

d. neither of the above

How interesting to you is the topic of this item? ____

60. When persons who are found not guilty by reason of insanity are eventually released they usually ____.
   a. commit crimes of greater severity than the original one
   b. commit crimes of about the same severity as the original one
   c. commit no new crimes
   d. are usually found not guilty by reason of insanity for a new offence

How interesting to you is the topic of this item? ____

61. "Scared Straight" (Juvenile Awareness Project) is a programme which attempts to reduce juvenile delinquency by exposing young offenders to the harsh realities of prison life. It is named after the fact that inmates try to scare young offenders with their description of the horrors of prison life, so that they will go "straight". This programme has been shown to be ____ in reducing juvenile delinquency.
   a. 100% effective
   b. very effective
   c. moderately effective
   d. ineffective

How interesting to you is the topic of this item? ____

62. People who have the so-called Type A personality (aggressive, hostile, ambitious, competitive) are ____ to suffer heart attacks.
   a. guaranteed
   b. highly likely
   c. moderately likely
   d. unlikely

How interesting to you is the topic of this item? ____

63. When black and white defendants are tried on similar offences, blacks are ____ more likely to be found guilty and be given longer sentences than whites.
   a. no
   b. 1–10%
   c. 15–22%
   d. 25–35%

How interesting to you is the topic of this item ? ____

64. It is evening and growing dark, but there is just enough light to see some colour. A person approaches you, wearing a shirt of a solid colour. The colour will be most easy to identify correctly if it is? ____.
   a. red
   b. orange
   c. yellow
   d. blue

How interesting to you is the topic of this item? ____

65. Brainstorming is a group problem-solving situation in which members are encouraged to present as many solutions as possible, no matter how unusual they might seem. Members are not permitted to criticize any ideas, but they are encouraged to elaborate on them. When compared to an appropriate control group of people working along, brainstorming has been shown to be
    a. much better
    b. somewhat better
    c. about as good
    d. worse

How interesting to you is the topic of this item? ____

Here are the correct answers:

1. A	2. D	3. C	4. C	5. A
6. D	7. A	8. C	9. B	10. C
11. D	12. D	13. C	14. C	15. B
16. C	17. A	18. D	19. C	20. D
21. C	22. D	23. C	24. D	25. B
26. D	27. D	28. A	29. A	30. A
31. C	32. A	33. D	34. D	35. B
36. A	37. B	38. C	39. D	40. D
41. B	42. A	43. A	44. B	45. C
46. A	47. A	48. C	49. A	50. D
51. B	52. D	53. C	54. C	55. C
56. C	57. B	58. D	59. D	60. C
61. D	62. D	63. B	64. D	65. D

Total your answers. How did you do? We would expect a psychology student to get about 50, and an intelligent lay person somewhere between 20 and 35. Certainly all of these issues and topics are examined in a psychology course. Do you still think psychology is just common sense? How highly did you score on the "interestingness" ratings? If there were a lot of 4s or 5s, a psychology course might be just what you are looking for. Which of the answers you got wrong were you most surprised about? Those topics might be an excellent starting point for your further reading.

What do employers think of psychology students?

There are at present about 2,000 graduates in psychology in Britain each year, and of these about three-quarters do not go on to become professional psychologists, but compete with graduates in other subjects in the non-specialist job market. A training in understanding human behaviour should equip them particularly well to do so, but it seems that there is still a long way to go in changing people's (especially employers's) prejudices about what a psychology course involves.

In a competitive situation, it is important to understand how employers regard psychology graduates. They know the average degree course lasts for three years but they do not know its content. Such evidence as there is about the general public's view of psychology suggests considerable ignorance of what psychology undergraduates study and that they are trained in a range of skills covering the arts, humanities and sciences. Various studies have reported that employers valued arts/humanities graduates for their critical skills and relevant knowledge, numeracy, ability to absorb information and analytic skills; scientists and engineers for relevant knowledge, numeracy, drive and ambition; and social scientists for communication skills, critical skills, ability to absorb information, and ambition. In addition, many employers also valued an ability to work with other people.

In a recent British study three occupational psychologists (Fletcher et al. 1991) asked 132 recruiters of psychology graduates what they thought about psychology versus humanities versus science graduates. The results are shown in Table 1.2.

Further analysis showed that compared to other graduates psychology graduates were rated higher in terms of being *people-oriented*, good at *colleague relations*, and high on *leadership*, but low on *logical numerical skills*, *mature poise* and *drive*. The data here suggest that, as far as employers are concerned, psychology graduates are still seen not as having the best of the both worlds, but rather the strengths of neither. Moreover, getting the lowest rating on attributes like *business knowledge, having values sympathetic to business, ambition and career orientation* and *knowing what they want from life* scarcely bodes well for their prospects of getting picked for a job in many private sector organizations. It is to be hoped that as employers become more accustomed to having psychologists in their workforce they will gain a more realistic notion of the skills and abilities which their training gives them.

The stereotype of the psychologist – when given a chance to show itself – is alive and well. Graduates in this discipline are seen as being people-orientated and as possessing such attributes as sensitivity, and the ability to understand and assess others and to help them with their problems. Their other attributes are overlooked.

Beware the fortune cookie

Is psychology as scientific as astrology or graphology? More people in fact seem to believe in astrology than psychology. But not only are they wrong, they are gullible to some of the oldest tricks in the trade.

Why do so many people from all backgrounds believe in, consult and act upon astrological and graphological predictions, despite the

Table 1.2 Interviewers' ratings of graduate groups on attributes (mean ratings).

	Psy.	Hum.	Science	
		Graduates		
**	3.5	3.55	3.2	leadership (1)
**	3.81	3.70	4.01	intellectual ability (2)
**	3.06	3.13	3.58	know what they want from life (3)
**	3.69	3.74	3.05	flexible and adaptable (4)
***	4.03	3.54	2.72	ability to deal with people's problems (5)
***	3.20	2.77	4.52	numeracy (6)
**	3.51	3.52	3.25	team-orientated (7)
**	3.10	3.20	3.63	appropriate respect for authority (8)
**	3.72	3.71	3.92	ability to work independently (9)
***	3.03	2.48	4.26	computing knowledge and skills (10)
	3.46	3.41	3.55	capacity to tolerate pressure (11)
**	3.44	3.60	3.10	putting across a good image (12)
**	3.65	3.77	3.20	imaginative approach; lots of ideas (13)
***	3.94	3.76	3.86	face-to-face communication skills (14)
	3.36	3.29	3.17	sufficiently mature to exercise authority (15)
***	3.60	3.86	2.98	can write well (reports, letters, etc.) (16)
**	3.31	3.44	3.73	career-orientated; ambitious (17)
**	3.63	3.74	3.32	fit in with others easily (18)
***	4.03	3.45	2.85	know what makes people tick (19)
	3.40	3.37	3.54	common sense (20)
	3.37	3.48	3.43	self-confident and emotionally stable (21)
***	3.88	3.99	2.82	can sum up other people well (22)
***	3.40	3.12	4.19	analytical; good at problem solving (23)
**	3.02	3.13	3.9	have values that are sympathetic to the world of business (24)
**	3.27	3.33	3.46	high drive, energetic and quick (25)
	3.32	3.42	3.23	not too academic or ivory-tower in approach (26)
***	3.66	2.62	4.14	knowledge of statistical techniques (27)
	3.63	3.78	3.78	trainable (28)
	3.16	3.01	3.31	ability to use a word processor (29)
***	3.90	3.63	2.89	sensitivity to others (30)
**	3.12	3.16	3.45	well informed about the job applied for (31)
*	2.78	2.95	2.93	business knowledge (32)
***	3.21	2.50	4.35	understanding of scientific principles (33)
***	3.80	3.13	2.42	counselling skills (34)
**	3.41	3.38	3.13	have values that fit in well with the public sector (35)

Ratings: 5 = very satisfactory; 1 = unsatisfactory
Significance differences:
*** psychology graduates differ from both other groups
** psychology graduates differ from science graduates only
* psychology graduates differ from humanities graduates only

latter's irreconcilability with either scientific rationalism or Christian beliefs, as well as a highly dubious reliability record? Some businesses in Britain use the services of a graphologist while the French frequently consult astrologers. Social scientists have considered seriously the possibility that there is some validity in these predictions, yet patient research on the part of impartial researchers has by and large failed to find any replicable theoretically based or explicable significant findings. This is perhaps far more true of graphology than of astrology for which there is equivocal evidence. Both are falsifiable and both have been falsified, yet people still believe in them. In short, graphology and astrology are bunk. Yet so many people are hoodwinked. Why?

There are two sorts of answers to this question. One concerns the reliability and validity of alternative, more acceptable, ways of assessing, describing or measuring people. High unemployment has meant unprecedented numbers of people applying for jobs and bewildered selectors are turning to any means of assessment that they can trust. Some believe in *school grades* or the predictiveness of leisure pursuits (always the source of greatest lies in an application form) despite the evidence that they are weak predictors of occupational success. Indeed, there is some evidence to suggest that there may be a reverse correlation between success in some A-level subjects (e.g. geography, drama studies) and occupational competence and promotion. Others have consulted *occupational psychologists* whose carefully constructed psychometric tests certainly have the appearance of objective scientific measures. However, British distrust of psychology, the emergence of numerous fairly bogus consultancies, and the excessive use of poorly psychometrized tests means that both because of the costs and the poor performance of some of these tests, distraught and overburdened selectors are turning elsewhere. Many have turned to *graphology*. Newspaper reports frequently quote a number of important, influential and possibly intelligent people who believe in, and hence use, graphology in selection. This is the case despite literally dozens of scientific studies that again and again challenge the validity of graphology to accurately describe personality or predict behaviour (e.g. Beyerstein & Beyerstein 1992).

However, the more plausible reason why people believe in graphology and astrology is paradoxical. People believe in graphological and astrological "interpretations" or "readings" because they are true but, and it is an important *but*, they are true because they consist of vague positive generalizations with high base-rate validity (i.e., they are true of most people) yet are supposedly derived specifically for a named person.

For nearly forty years psychologists have been investigating the Barnum Effect. It was the famous circus-act producer Phineas T. Barnum who said "There's a sucker born every minute" and had as his formula of success "A little something for everybody". The Barnum Effect refers to the phenomenon whereby people accept personality feedback about themselves, whether it is universally valid or trivial, because it is supposedly derived from personality assessment procedures. In other words, people believe in astrology and graphology because they fall victim to the fallacy of personal validation, which means that people accept the generalizations, the trite bogus descriptions which are true of nearly everybody, to be specifically true of themselves.

Consider a psychological study to illustrate this point. An American psychologist called Stagner gave a group of personnel managers a well-established personality test. But instead of scoring it and giving them the actual results, he gave each of them bogus feedback in the form of 13 statements derived from horoscopes, graphological analyses and so on. Each manager was then asked to read over the feedback (supposedly derived for him/herself from the "scientific" test) and decide how accurate the assessment was by marking each sentence on a scale (a) Amazingly accurate, (b) Rather good, (c) About half and half, (d) More wrong than right, (e) Almost entirely wrong. Table 1.3 shows the results – over half felt their profile was an amazingly accurate description of them, while 40 per cent thought it was rather good. Almost none believed it to be very wrong.

A glance at the items reveals exactly the process. If you add together the first two columns and look at those two items considered *most accurate* ("You prefer a certain amount of change and variety and become dissatisfied when hemmed in by restrictions and limitations" and "While you have some personality weaknesses, you are generally able to compensate for them") and *least accurate* ("Your sexual adjustment has presented problems for you" and "Some of your aspirations tend to be pretty unrealistic") you see the importance of positive general feedback. People definitely and not unnaturally have a penchant for the positive. Many researchers have replicated this result. A French psychologist advertised his services as an astrologer in various newspapers and got back hundreds of requests for his services. He replied to each letter by sending out mimeographed identical copies of a single, ambiguous "horoscope". More than 200 clearly gullible clients actually wrote back praising his accuracy and perceptiveness. An Australian professor regularly gets his first year students to write down in frank detail their dreams, or he might ask them to describe in detail what they see in an inkblot – the more mystical the task, the better. A week later he gives them the 13 statements shown in the table and gets them to rate them. Only after they have publicly declared their belief in the test are they encouraged to swop feedback. The humiliation of being so easily fooled is a powerful learning experience.

Research on the Barnum Effect has, however, shown that beliefs in

Table 1.3 Evaluation of items by 68 personnel managers when presented as a "personality" analysis.

	Judgement as to accuracy of item percent[1] choosing				
	a[2]	b	c	d	e
A. You have a great need for other people to like and admire you.	39	46	13	1	1
B. You have a tendency to be critical of yourself.	46	36	15	3	0
C. You have a great deal of unused capacity which you have not turned to your advantage.	37	36	18	1	4
D. While you have some personality weaknesses, you are generally able to compensate for them.	34	55	9	0	0
E. Your sexual adjustment has presented problems for you.	15	16	16	33	19
F. Disciplined and self-controlled outside, you tend to be worrisome and insecure inside.	40	21	22	10	4
G. At times you have serious doubts as to whether you have made the right decision or done the right thing.	37	31	9	18	4
H. You prefer a certain amount of change and variety and become dissatisfied when hemmed in by restriction and limitations.	63	28	7	1	1
I You pride yourself as an independent thinker and do not accept others' statements without satisfactory proof.	49	32	12	4	4
J. You have found it unwise to be frank in revealing yourself to others.	31	37	22	6	4
K. At time you are extroverted, affable, sociable, while at other times you are introverted, wary, reserved.	43	25	18	9	5
L. Some of your aspirations tend to be pretty unrealistic.	12	16	22	43	7
M. Security is one of your major goals in life.	40	31	15	9	5

[1] Not all percentages add to 100% because of omissions by an occasional subject.
[2] Definitions of scale steps as follows:
  a. amazingly accurate
  b. rather good
  c. about half and half
  d. more wrong than right
  e. almost entirely wrong

this bogus feedback is influenced by a number of important factors, some to do with the client and the consultant (their personality or naïvety) and some to do with the nature of the test and the feedback situation itself. Curiously, client (naïve purchaser) and consultant (astrologer, graphologer) factors have shown comparatively few results. Women are not more susceptible than men, although of course generally naïve or gullible people are (tautologically!) more susceptible to this effect. Furthermore, the status, prestige of the consultant is only marginally important, which is of course good news for the more bogus people in this field.

However, some variables are crucial. One of the most important is *perceived specificity* of the information required. The more detailed the question, the better – so you have to specify exact time, date and place of birth to astrologers. In one study an American researcher gave all his subjects the same horoscope and found that those who were told that the interpretation was based on the year, month and day of birth judged it to be more accurate than those who were led to believe that it was based only on the year and month. Again and again, studies show that after people receive general statements they think *pertain just to them* their faith in the procedure and in the diagnostician increases. A client's satisfaction is no measure of how well the diagnostician has differentiated him or her from others but it is utterly dependent on the extent to which they believe it is specific to them.

The second factor belies the truth that we are all hungry for compliments but sceptical of criticism. That is, the feedback must be favourable. It need not be entirely, utterly positive but if it is by and large positive with the occasional mildly negative comment (that itself may be a compliment) people will believe it. This can easily be demonstrated by presenting the well-used 13 statements in the table with the opposite, primarily negative, meaning (i.e. "You do not pride yourself as an independent thinker and accept others' statements without satisfactory proof"). People do not readily accept the negative version even if it is seemingly specifically tailored to them. This confirms another principle in personality measurement – the "Pollyanna Principle" which suggests that there is an universal human tendency to use or accept positive words or feedback more frequently, diversely and facilely than negative words and feedback. It has been shown that according to the evaluation of two judges there were five times as many favourable as unfavourable statements in highly acceptable interpretations and twice as many unfavourable statements in rarely accepted interpretations.

It is not difficult to explain the popularity of astrology and graphology. The lengthy feedback is based on *specific information* (time and place of birth for astrology; slant and size of writing, correctness of letters, dotting of i's and crossing of t's and use of loops in graphology). It is nearly always favourable. Take for example the analysis of a prominent British politician's writing published in a quality newspaper: "Optimistic, forward-looking. Extrovert, intelligent. Appreciative of the arts. Cultured. Decisive. Signs of stubbornness. Quick mind, but not good with trivia; needs people to whom he can delegate" – a typical example of general positive statements applicable to between five and ten million people in this country. And note the praising with faint damns – "Signs of stubbornness" (rather than "Signs of intelligence" and "Stubborn") and "not good with trivia". Also, it is often the *troubled* (worried, depressed, insecure) who visit astrologers, graphologists, fortune tellers. They are particularly sensitive to objective positive information about themselves and the future. Therefore, the very type of feedback and the predisposition of clients make the acceptance highly probable. This also accounts for the popularity of astrological books; "Your stars foretell" columns in books; the I Ching, etc. Each offers fairly long descriptions of each sun sign type in positive general terms but with the caveat and a warning that the description is only an approximation and that an accurate description can solely be obtained from a specifically cast horoscope. But if the general description seems true (and it probably is), people frequently conclude that it must be even more true when even more specific information is used. Furthermore, this process is enhanced over time for two reasons. Since Freud, it has been known that people selectively remember more positive events about themselves than negative ones and are thus likely to remember more feedback that coincides with their own view of themselves than information that is less relevant or contradicted it. Secondly, of course, people have to pay for the consultation. Perhaps one needs a wealth warning in every astrological statement.

There are other attractions of astrological and graphical readings. They not only give useful, "fascinating" information about oneself, but they are also claimed to predict the future, so reducing anxieties and uncertainties about what will happen. Also, unlike other forms of therapy which require psychological work and/or behaviour change to obtain any benefit, in graphology one merely has to supply a writing specimen, in astrology the exact time and place of birth. There is much to gain and little to lose at the astrol-graphologist. Not surprisingly then a comfortable collaborative illusion of scientific validity emerges formed between the buyer and seller of the astrological reading and handwriting analyses.

Finally, there is one other reason why people validate graphology and astrology – the self-fulfilling prophecy. It is quite possible that if one is told "As a Virgo, you are particularly honest", this may lead one to notice and subsequently selectively recall all or any, albeit trivial instances of behavioural confirmation (pointing out that a person had dropped a bus ticket; giving back excess change). The self-fulfilling prophecy may work on both a conceptual and a behavioural basis. Thus Virgos come to include the trait of honesty in their self-concept but also they may actually become slightly or occasionally more honest. Thus, graphology and astrology predictions may come true because accepting the predictions partly dictates that our behaviour will change appropriately!

Beware the fortune cookie, the graphologist, the astrologer! The moral of the story, of course, is that you can impress anyone with the perspicacity of your psychological insights as long as they are vague, relevant for most people, generally favourable, but personalized just for that other person. Fortune tellers have exploited this fact for hundreds of years. Crystal balls have been replaced by tarot cards or simple pen and ink, but the principle remains the same: "The fault of false belief, dear reader, is not in our stars, it is in ourselves."

Psychology is not just common sense. Psychologists study common sense and attempt, through their research, to answer which of different, often contradictory, common-sense ideas are true.

Chapter 2
Background and history of psychology

Introduction

Some people, usually lawyers or essay writers, like to start with definitions. You may have noticed that we didn't, but we cannot put off this particular issue any longer. Unfortunately, although they are not difficult to find, rather different definitions of psychology exist and it is not certain how useful they are.

There is a story, possibly a myth, concerning the folly of seeking out and relying too heavily on definitions. A young man had been appointed to a lectureship at a famous university and he was fortunate in having six months before assuming the job to prepare all his lectures. He was given the "Introduction to Psychology" class as his major teaching task and he thought it might be a good idea to begin with defining what psychology is (and is not). It soon became apparent to him that this was a difficult task – at least to get right – but he determined to carry on until he got a comprehensive and correct definition. But it took so long that by the time term had begun he still had not finished the first part of the first lecture – the definition.

Definitions that have been proposed include the *science of the mind, the scientific study of behaviour,* and *the study of mental experience.* The problem is really that because psychology is such a diverse discipline, as we shall see, with many different branches, it is rather difficult to come up with just one simple but comprehensive definition.

However, as Colman (1988) has suggested, it is important to say what psychology is not; that is to describe related disciplines that are essentially different from, but occasionally confused with, psychology. They are:

- *Psychiatry.* A branch of medicine that specializes in the prevention, diagnosis and treatment of mental illness. Psychologists are not usually medically trained; psychiatrists always are. Clinical psychologists are often interested in the same phenomena as psychiatrists but tend to develop different theories of their cause or methods for treatment.

- *Psychoanalysis.* This is a theory of mental life (both structure and function) and a method of psychotherapy devised by Sigmund Freud. It places heavy emphasis on unconscious processes. It also involves a lengthy training process. Some psychologists and psychiatrists go on to become psychoanalysts but they make up a small percentage of the total.
- *Psychometrics.* This is the study of mental testing and involves the development and validation of aptitude, ability and attitude, IQ and personality tests. It is a small but important branch of psychology.
- *Parapsychology.* This is the study of paranormal behaviour, particularly extra-sensory perception (ESP) and psychokinesis. It has a long history and is dedicated to the difficult and painstaking research, sometimes conducted by psychologists, that looks particularly for the evidence for ESP. However, many psychologists are dismissive of this branch of psychology, pointing to very few replicable findings from all the research done.

Different approaches to psychology

For all sorts of reasons – what they are studying, how they have been trained, what their theories are – psychologists tend to be attracted to different approaches in psychology. While most psychologists tend to have a basic leaning towards one or another of these philosophies, they generally borrow from all. In fact, it would be rare to find a psychologist who sticks to only one of the approaches discussed below. There are five broad approaches to explaining behaviour: the behavioural, the phenomenological/humanistic, the psychoanalytic, the cognitive, and the neurobiological.

- *The behavioural approach.* Behaviourists believe that humans or animals are the end product of whatever has happened to them in their interaction with the environment: a product of basic learning from the various stimuli (and responses) they have been exposed to. Thus, the criminal is the end product of learning bad habits; and the altruist the opposite. Stimuli from the environment and reactions to them are the most important predictors of behaviour. If you have a moral environment, you have a good person; an immoral environment equals a bad person; a good mother and father to imitate results in a good child, and so forth. The basic position held is that we are what we learn to be. Change the environment and you also change the end product. Most behaviourists pay little attention to the inner workings or thoughts/feelings/motives of individuals, preferring to focus on observable behaviour. Behaviourists believe that observable phenomena (that is behaviours that you can see and measure) are the *stuff* of psychological science, rather than say, unconscious wishes or beliefs which one cannot directly observe.

- *The phenomenological/humanistic approach.* In direct contrast to the behaviourists are psychologists who emphasize mental processes occurring inside the person as a basic force for explaining human behaviour. The word "phenomenon", in this context, refers to events that are forever changing, never remaining the same. The phenomenologists argue that no matter what is happening in the environment, each person is so unique that what is finally seen or understood from that environment is changed or altered by the person to fit his or her own beliefs or needs. The term humanistic comes from humane, or a belief in the basic goodness of people, and suggests that by our very nature we are capable of reaching perfection.

  The criminal, then, develops poor behaviour patterns because the environment doesn't provide the proper atmosphere for growth and development. It blocks personal development, and we are destined to be good, useful people; so the humanists believe. The distinction between the phenomenologists and the behaviourists is that for the former group, growth is internal, or inside the human, and this growth will go on unless the environment is very difficult and stifling. Also, growth is very individual; that is, each person is very special and very different from every other person. For humanistic psychologists people have one thing in common – they are all different!

  Humanists believe individuals can become whatever they wish. The important aspect is the emotional interpretation that each of us gives to what happens in the environment. The death of a parent has a different meaning for individual A than it has for individual B. This is because each of us has different internal experiences we bring to bear on the outside event. Compared to the behaviourists' view, the outside event is of secondary importance; humanists focus almost exclusively on the inner working of the person.

- *The psychoanalytic approach.* While the phenomenologists/humanists believe in the essential goodness of the human being, the psychoanalysts by and large emphasize the primitive animal nature within us. Psychoanalysts emphasize an inner self preoccupied with sex, aggression and basic bodily needs, all of which operate at the unconscious level. As we don't know what is in the unconscious, we don't know what is causing our behaviour. This particular philosophy started with Sigmund Freud who maintained that we seek only self-gratification. It should be noted, however, that today's followers of psychoanalysis have tempered Freud's basic beliefs because they seemed too extreme. In any case, psycho-analysts stand in stark contrast to the humanistic group. The Freudian view is that often unconscious motives, needs and drives determine our behaviour and often symbolic fears and even physical illness are the direct result of unconsciousness conflict.

– *The cognitive approach.* The cognitive psychologists emphasize thought processes, reasoning and problem solving. For cognitive psychology, the most important human ability is our capacity to take information from the environment, analyze this information in a systematic way, and come up with a solution to a problem. Cognitive psychologists stress that we are thinking creatures who often make mistakes, able to compare things we have seen in the past with what we are presently seeing and thus able to make judgements about them. Their aim is to develop a model or theory of human operations that we can then examine to see if it is correct. In this regard, behaviourism is too mechanical for the cognitivists: it deals, they believe, with the carpenter's tools rather than the carpenter. Humanism is too vague for them because it leaves everything to a process that is not clear. The cognitivists say they have a working model of human thought and this model is an elaborate, organized theory of how we process information. We take in material from the environment, match it to our past experiences, search the categories in our brain for additional information, compare what we have with what we got, and arrive at a decision.

– *The neurobiological approach.* There are two different ways of understanding the response a person might have to some kind of event in the physical environment. One way is to view the situation as primarily psychological (literally related to the mind) and the other is to see the response as neuro- (nerve cells) biological (physical; including chemical, muscular). Consider a person fleeing from a bird (ornithophobia). Some psychologists focus on the background and learning experiences of this individual in order to explain the behaviour. Neurobiologists take a different approach. They describe the behaviour in terms of the neurobiological changes that are taking place in the person as the result of previous experiences. For example, the person has learned to become terrified by pigeons in the past, and seeing a pigeon in the present triggers the same set of physical alterations (chemicals in the blood, heart-rate changes, sweating, etc.) that occurred in the earlier experiences. Neurobiologists are interested in the biological foundations of behaviour and tend to focus on physiological processes.

There are also other approaches like the *ethological* or *evolutionary* approach which looks at the development and change of behaviour over time. It relies on the Darwinian ideas of natural selection.

How do the various approaches understand the same problem, in this case that of a failure of memory? Consider the everyday problem of John Smith. John is 40 years old and lives with his mother. He has never been married, but has friends and a good job as an accountant. His life seemed to have been going reasonably well – or so he thought. During the last six months, however, John has become depressed and he is forgetting things. He had always remembered his mother's birthday, but this year he completely forgot about it, which hurt her considerably. He met a woman he really liked, set up a date with her a week later, only to discover that he was going to be out of town during that time. So, to his embarrassment, he had to cancel it. Usually pretty logical and methodical he is clearly not himself. He has become very quiet, introspective and scatty.

- *Behavioural analysis.* According to the behaviourists, when John was a child he was consoled by his mother rather than scolded when he did things wrong. Not only was he rewarded by her attention, but she encouraged him to stay home because he was ill. The behaviourists might then argue that John has learned very bad habits. He is currently unhappy with his life – for whatever reason – and is using the same behaviour that worked in the past to get attention, only instead of forgetting books, he is forgetting other things. He has, in short, learned the benefits of forgetting, and is trying to attract sympathy and help.

- *Phenomenological/humanistic analysis.* In the view of phenomenologists and humanists, John is destined to continue with his work as an accountant. But John's inner world has suffered a number of blows because things have not been going right, and he is more and more distracted. While some might guess John is feeling conflict, we don't know this because such a general statement could apply to many people. We have to find out what it is specifically that bothers John. It will be something in a poor environment causing him to lose steam in his personal development. Every effort will be made to understand him and to realign his environment into a more fitting setting for his goals. We have to know how he currently sees his life situation.

- *Psychoanalytic analysis.* For the psychoanalysts, who emphasize basic needs such as sex and aggression and unconscious motives, John may be suffering from a classic conflict of wanting a relationship with this new woman friend as well as his mother. Thus, John is trying to keep the two "love affairs" going at the same time. This may not be working because he is becoming frustrated in his desires and hence becoming more aggressive, as when his unconscious causes him to forget his mother's birthday. The longer this goes on, the more John feels guilty; the more guilty he becomes, the more aggressive he becomes. The more aggressive he becomes, the more he strikes out at others by "forgetting". His forgetting is a "solution" to the conflict.

- *Cognitive analysis.* Cognitive psychologists focus on current thinking skills rather than on previous learning or unconscious impulses. Thus, the cognitivists would get John to analyze exactly what his life is like, and what kinds of things he is saying to himself that are not reasonable. They would probably focus on what, when and how he forgets particular things and how he tries to remember. He may have inappropriate strategies or poor methods of remembering and techniques to rectify these can easily be taught to him. John will have to make a formal, logical plan of action to improve his life at home, at work, and in his relationship with the woman and his mother. Then, they claim, his memory will improve all by itself.
- *Neurobiological analysis.* One of the keys to an active memory is a reasonably high level of activating chemicals in the brain. Thus, if we are excited, we firmly lock into our memory the event that brought about the excitement. But John is showing symptoms that are just the opposite: he has been depressed much of the time lately. This depression is lowering the level of activating chemicals necessary for useful day-to-day remembering. So, John's problem may be explained by the neurobiologists by focusing on chemical events and physiological changes.

Of course, it is possible that a psychologist may favour a combination of approaches. But the above everyday example shows how psychologists from the different branches of psychology focus on quite different factors and offer different explanations.

Some early thinkers

One way to understand the origin or history of a discipline is to study the lives and thoughts of the original thinkers. Morris (1978) described half a dozen of the most famous founding fathers of the discipline of psychology nearly all working in the last decades of the nineteenth century or between 1900 and 1930.

Wundt and Titchener: structuralism and the emergence of psychology

In 1879 Wilhelm Wundt (1832–1920) opened the first psychological laboratory in Europe at the University of Leipzig in Germany. He was in fact Professor of Philosophy (not Psychology) from 1875 to 1920. Wundt had written *Principles of physiological psychology* in 1874 and he argued that "The mind must be studied objectively and scientifically". Wundt refused to see the mind or human behaviour in "mystical" terms. Thinking, he argued, is a natural event like wind in a storm or the beating of the heart. By 1879, the scientific method he proposed commanded great respect in the academic community.

By the mid-1880s Wundt's new psychological lab had many students. His main concern at this point was with techniques for uncovering the natural laws of the human mind. To find the basic units of thought, he began by looking at perception. When we look at an object like an orange, for example, we immediately think, here is a fruit, something to peel and eat. But these are associations. All we really see is a round orange object.

Wundt and his co-workers wanted to strip perception of its associations, to find the very atoms of thought. They trained themselves in the art of objective *introspection*, observing and recording their perceptions and feelings. They introduced measurement and experiments into psychology, which until this time had been a branch of philosophy.

Psychology became the science of consciousness – the physics of the mind. In physics an hour or a mile is an exact measure. Could the same precision be achieved in psychology? Psychology is the study of experience. Students of Wundt, notably Edward Bradford Titchener (1867–1927), broke experience down into three basic elements: physical sensations (including sights and sounds); affections or feelings (which are like sensations, but less clear); and images (such as memories and dreams). When we recognize an orange, according to Titchener's scheme, we combine a physical sensation (what we see) with feelings (liking or disliking oranges) and with images (memories of other oranges). Even the most complex thoughts and feelings, Titchener argued, can be reduced to these simple elements. Psychology's role is to identify the elements and show how they are combined. Because it stresses the basic units of experience and the combinations in which they occur, this school of psychology is called structuralism.

Perhaps the most important product of the Leipzig lab was its students; they took the science to universities around the world. Among them was Titchener. British by birth but German in training and temperament, Titchener became the leader of American psychology soon after he became Professor of Psychology at Cornell University, a post he held until his death in 1927.

In Britain, University College London made important contributions to psychology as the subject emerged as a separate discipline in the nineteenth century. Early interest in the research aspects of psychology was stimulated by the work of individuals from several different departments.

In 1837 Professor John Elliotson pioneered the use of mesmerism (hypnotism) during surgical operations at University College Hospital: Charles Dickens was among those who attended some of his demonstrations. Another medical pioneer, this time in the field of psychiatry, was Henry Maudsley who was Professor of Medical Jurisprudence at University College from 1869 to 1879 and editor of *The Journal of Mental Science*.

Sir Francis Galton's (1822–1911) work is fundamental to large areas of contemporary psychology, particularly to the fields of differential psychology and psychometrics, and we shall return to consider his contribution more fully in the next section. For the moment we should mention that he was the first to investigate and measure individual differences in human abilities and traits. He provided evidence that such traits might be largely inherited in man, and he was the first to employ the statistical technique of correlation to assess the relationship between measured qualities. The Eugenics Record Office, which he established in Gower Street, London in 1904 was the precursor of the Galton Laboratory at University College.

Contrasted with Germany and the United States, scientific psychology had a very slow and somewhat painful birth in Britain despite the pioneering efforts of Elliotson, Maudsley, Galton and others. The idea that human behaviour is lawful, and that it is possible to discover these laws by the use of scientific methods is capable of producing deep passion. In 1877 James Ward proposed that a laboratory should be established in Cambridge to study psychophysics (the relation between the physical properties of stimuli and experienced sensations). This proposal was indignantly rejected by the Cambridge Senate on the grounds that it "would insult religion by putting the human soul in a pair of scales". This attitude and its derivations have taken a long time to die.

Psychology of a philosophic type in the tradition of British empiricism has been effectively taught at University College since the appointment of Croom Robertson to the Grote Chair of Mind and Logic in 1866. In his Inaugural Lecture, Robertson expressed the view that "psychology is the most fundamental and representative part of philosophy". He also believed, paradoxically, that "our psychology should be as physiological as we can make it".

It was Robertson's successor, Sully, who first introduced experimental work, and the establishment of a psychological laboratory in 1897 was an important landmark in the history of British psychology. It was founded only some eighteen years after the first ever psychological laboratory was established by Wundt in Leipzig in 1879. In the July 1897 issue of the journal *Mind* the following notice appeared:

A laboratory for experimental psychology will be opened in University College London in October next. The committee have secured a considerable part of the apparatus collected by Professor Hugo Munsterberg of Freiburg, who is about to migrate permanently to Harvard College. Among those who have contributed to the movement are Mr F Galton, Professor H Sidgwick, Mr A J Balfour, Mr R B Haldane, Sir John Lubbock, Mr Shadworth Hodgson and Dr Savage. It is hoped that the name of George Croom Robertson may in some way be connected with the laboratory. It is further hoped that Dr W H R Rivers whose work as a teacher in Cambridge and elsewhere is well known will be able to start the work of the laboratory and superintend it during the October term.

The claim of being the first psychological laboratory in Britain is sometimes disputed by Cambridge where Michael Foster, the Professor of Physiology, set aside one room for studies of the special senses in the same year. The Psychological Laboratory at Cambridge was founded in 1901. But both universities responded with characteristic British caution to such a new discipline. Each university allotted one room to the subject and Rivers was put in charge of both laboratories.

Earlier, in 1892 the Second International Congress of Psychology met in London at University College with Professor Sully as one of the two joint secretaries. In 1900 William McDougall was appointed to a part-time Readership in Experimental Psychology in Sully's department. Of this period Dr May Smith writes: "During this time he used to hold informal discussions in his laboratory and gathered there a small group of people interested in psychology". This group formed the nucleus of the British Psychological Society which was formally inaugurated at University College on 24 October 1901.

Sir Francis Galton: individual differences

In Britain, as we have noted above, Francis Galton, Charles Darwin's half-cousin, was dabbling in medicine. Throughout his life, he remained an intellectual adventurer – to the great gain of psychology. Galton was a pioneer in the development of mental tests and the study of individual differences. He was impressed by the number of exceptional people in his own family and studied the histories of other families. His research suggested that genius might be hereditary. Intrigued, Galton invented tests to measure individual capacities and worked out ways of comparing scores, testing people at the Science Museum in London. He found a wide range of abilities and complex relations between one ability and another. Later he became interested in mental imagery and word association.

Francis Galton was also fascinated by the concept of genius. To determine its hereditary basis, he studied family biographies and other accounts of eminent people. He concluded that since outstanding intellectual ability occurred more frequently among the close relatives of eminent people than it did among remote ones, the origins of intelligence were surely genetic. The flaw in Galton's observations, as well as in many similar contemporary conclusions, is that they fail to tell us whether genetics is truly responsible. Eminent persons very likely do provide their offspring with a superior genetic endowment, but then they also usually provide them with superior educational, cultural and learning opportunities as well. Thus, the effects of heredity and environment remain tightly intertwined.

More sophisticated studies have investigated intelligence in fraternal and identical twins. Identical twins share exactly the same genetic background whereas fraternal twins are no more likely to be similar genetically than ordinary siblings. Clearly, then, if genetics is important one would expect the IQs of identical twins to be more alike than those of fraternal twins. Indeed, that is exactly the case.

William James: functionalism

William James (1842–1910), the first important American-born psychologist, originally studied chemistry, physiology, anatomy, biology and medicine. Then, in 1872, he accepted an offer to teach physiology at Harvard. There, James read philosophy in his free time and saw a link between it and physiology. The two seemed to converge in psychology.

In 1875 James began a class in psychology and set aside part of his laboratory for psychological experiments. He also began work on a text, *The principles of psychology*, which was published in 1890.

In preparing his lectures and textbook, James studied structuralist writings thoroughly and decided that something in Wundt's and Titchener's approach was wrong. He concluded that the atoms of experience – pure sensations without associations – did not exist. Consciousness, he believed, was a continuous flow, not an assemblage of bits of sensation and pieces of imagery. Perceptions and associations, sensations and emotions, cannot be separated.

James turned to the study of habit and argued that much of what we do is automatic. We do not have to think about how to do everyday things. James suggested that when we repeat something several times, our nervous systems are changed, so that each time we open a door, the action is performed more easily than it was the last time. Thus, mental associations allow us to benefit from previous experience. Once we have solved a problem, the solution becomes automatic. This, James argued, is the essence of adaptation.

With *The principles of psychology* James thus forged a new link between psychology and natural science. Applying biological principles to the mind, he arrived at a functionalist theory of mental life and behaviour. Functionalist theory is concerned, for example, not just with learning, sensation or perception, but rather with how an organism uses its learning or sensory and perceptual abilities to function in its environment. James also argued for the value of subjective (untrained) introspection and insisted that psychology focus on everyday experiences.

John B. Watson: behaviourism

J. B. Watson (1878–1958), another American, graduated from the University of Chicago and later worked at Johns Hopkins University. Watson's PhD was on learning in rats. (In fact students still refer to psychology, rather unfairly, as "all rats and stats".) One of the department's requirements was that he speculate on the kind of consciousness that produced the behaviour he observed in his experiments. Watson found this ridiculous and doubted that rats had any consciousness at all. Ten years and many experiments later Watson was ready to confront both the structuralist and functionalist schools. In *Psychology as the behaviourist views it* (1913) he argued that the whole idea of consciousness, of mental life, is simply superstition. Psychology must be the study of observable, measurable behaviour – and nothing more.

Watson's position was based largely on Ivan Pavlov's famous observation that the dogs in his laboratory began to salivate as soon as they heard their feeder coming – even before they could see their dinner. Pavlov had always thought that salivation was a natural response to food, and he found the dogs' anticipation odd. He decided to see if he could teach them to salivate in response to the sound of a tuning fork, even when no food was in the room. He did this successfully by first sounding the tuning fork just before the dogs saw and tasted food. He explained this as follows: all behaviour is a response to some stimulus in the environment. In ordinary life, food (the stimulus) makes dogs salivate (the response). All Pavlov did was to train (or "condition") his animals to expect food when they heard a new stimulus – a certain sound (the conditional stimulus).

In a famous experiment with an 11-month-old child, Watson showed that people can also be conditioned. Little Albert was a secure, happy baby who had no reason to fear soft, furry, white rats. Watson changed all that. Every time Albert reached out to pet the rat Watson hit a metal bar with a hammer, startling the child. Soon Albert was afraid not only of white rats but also of white rabbits, white dogs, white fur coats and Watson himself!

Watson saw no reason to refer to consciousness or mental life to explain this change. Little Albert, he argued, simply responded to the environment – in this case the coincidence of the loud noises and white, furry things. Watson felt the same was true for adults. Words, he argued, are simply a verbal response; when we think, we are really talking to ourselves; emotions are a glandular response, and all behaviour can be explained with the stimulus–response formula. Psychology, he felt, must be purged of "mentalism".

B. F. Skinner: S–R psychology

B. F. Skinner (1904–92), working at Harvard University, was one of the leaders of behaviourism. Like Watson, Skinner believed that psychology should only study observable and measurable behaviour. Skinner explained behaviour in terms of the stimulus–response formula. He too was primarily interested in changing behaviour through conditioning or learning – and discovering natural laws of behaviour in the process. But his approach was subtly different from that of his predecessor. Watson had changed little Albert's behaviour by changing the stimulus. As far as Albert knew, white rats made loud, scary noises. For Albert to learn this, Watson had had to repeat the experience over and over, making a loud noise every time Albert saw a rat. Skinner added a new element – reinforcement. He rewarded his subjects for behaving the way he wanted them to behave. For example, an animal (rats and pigeons were Skinner's favourite subjects) was put in a special cage (called a Skinner box) and allowed to explore. Eventually the animal would reach up and press a lever or peck at a disk on the wall. A food pellet then dropped into a box. Gradually the animal learned that pressing the bar or pecking at the disk always brought food. Why did the animal learn this? Because it had been reinforced, or rewarded. Skinner thus made the animal an active agent in its own conditioning. For this reason this type of learning is often referred to as instrumental learning.

Sigmund Freud: psychoanalytic psychology.

Sigmund Freud (1856–1939), originally a doctor in Vienna, was largely unknown outside continental Europe until the late 1920s, though he had been working and publishing papers for well over thirty years. By then he had worked his clinical observation into a comprehensive theory of mental life that differed radically from those of his American colleagues.

Freud believed much of our behaviour is governed by hidden motives and unconscious wishes. It is as if part of each of us never grows up. The adult in us struggles to control the infant, but with only partial success. Childish desires and wishes surface in mistakes called "Freudian slips" as well as in our dreams. We feel that many of our impulses are forbidden or sinful. Therefore, we do not want to admit them to our consciousness. Often this conflict leads to vague feelings of anxiety and sometimes to exaggerated fears.

Freud not only found that adult problems could be traced back to childhood experiences, but he also maintained that unconscious feelings were always sexual. A little boy, he argued, desires his mother and wants to destroy his rival – her husband and his father (the so-called Oedipus Conflict). Of all Freud's concepts, this – the idea of infant sexuality – was the most shocking, and many of Freud's own colleagues rejected his emphasis on sex. Alfred Adler, for example, felt the child's sense of inferiority in relation to "big people" was central to personality. Carl Jung emphasized self-realization (that is, self-discovery) in the context of the racial history and religious beliefs of the human species. Jung's ideas of the collective unconscious and of personality types is today very influential.

Nonetheless, Freudian theory had a huge impact on academic psychology (particularly on the study of personality), and it is still controversial. Some psychologists accept the theories of the unconscious, infantile sexuality and dream interpretation; others find them ridiculous. Freud's theory has probably influenced the arts, humanities and literature more than any other psychological theory, although his influence inside psychology is probably on the wane.

Some modern thinkers

Most of the more important psychologists, however, are alive and working today. In Britain three people in particular have shaped much of the discipline over the last twenty-five years. They are Michael Argyle, Donald Broadbent and Hans Eysenck. The following brief biographies give some indication of the extent of their contribution and influence.

Michael Argyle (1926–)

After serving in the RAF Argyle was educated at Emmanuel College, Cambridge and became a research student at the Cambridge Psychological Laboratory in 1950. In 1952 he was appointed University Lecturer in Social Psychology at Oxford, where he later became a Reader in Social Psychology and a Fellow of Wolfson College. During his career Argyle was a Fellow of the Centre for Advanced Study in the Behavioural Sciences at Stanford University in the USA, and was a visiting professor at a number of universities in the USA, Canada, Australia, Europe, Africa and Israel, and has been on lecture tours in other parts of the world. He has carried out a variety of research and consultancy projects especially in the areas of social skills training and selection and pioneered the use of social skills training in Britain. He has been awarded a series of research grants for work on social interaction, social skills, non-verbal communication and related topics and led an active research group at Oxford. Argyle's publications include *The scientific study of social behaviour* (1957), *Psychology and social problems* (1964), *The psychology of interpersonal behaviour* (1967, 1972, 1978, 1983), *Social interaction* (1969), *Bodily communication* (1975, 1988), *The social psychology of religion* (1975, with B. Beit-Hallahmi), *Gaze and mutual gaze* (1976, with Mary Cook), *Social skills and mental health* (1978, with P. Trower and B. Bryant), *Social situations* (1981, with A. Furnham and J. A. Graham), *The anatomy of relationships* (1985, with Monika Henderson), *The psychology of happiness* (1987) and many articles in British, American and European journals. He is famous for his sense of humour, his love of travelling and Scottish country dancing, and his belief that psychology can be put to good use to help people.

Donald Broadbent (1926–93)

Broadbent, who died in 1993, was Director of the Medical Research Council Applied Psychology Unit in Cambridge from 1958 to 1974, when he moved to Oxford in order to concentrate on research. Prior to this move he had to squeeze in his own research three afternoons a week between actually running the Unit. Before Oxford, Broadbent had spent all his academic career in Cambridge. When he came out of the RAF at the end of the Second World War, he studied psychology in Cambridge, believing he would go into industrial psychology, but the opportunity came along to do some research for the navy on the effects of noise. The noises that had to be used were too loud for the navy laboratories to bear so Broadbent did the research at the Applied Psychology Unit, using a deserted hangar some miles out of Cambridge to run his subjects who performed a variety of tasks while shrill white noise screamed at them. Broadbent wrote two important books, *Perception and communication* (1958) and *Decision and stress* (1971), in which he looked at the way the brain copes with information and the practical ways in which these findings could be applied. He also wrote two of the most lucid and persuasive arguments for what one might call an evolved behaviourism instead of old-time behaviourism. These books are *Behaviour* (1961) and *In defence of empirical psychology* (1974). *Behaviour* was a popular introduction which summarized what the behaviourist approach had enabled us to learn about man in the previous fifty years. *In defence of empirical psychology* contains the William James Memorial Lectures which Broadbent was invited to deliver at Harvard in 1972.

In *Behaviour*, Broadbent wrote:

> Nobody can grasp the nature of things from an armchair, and until fresh experiments have been performed we do not know what their results will be. The confident dogmatisms about human nature which fall so readily from pulpits, newspapers' editorials, and school prize givings are not for us. Rather we must

be prepared to live with an incomplete knowledge of behaviour but with confidence in the power of objective methods to give us that knowledge some day. (p. 201)

A man of charm and modesty, there is almost total agreement that Broadbent has been one of the greatest contributors to psychology.

Hans Eysenck (1916–)

Eysenck was born in 1916 and obtained his PhD degree in psychology at London University after school and university experience in Germany, France and England. Having worked as a psychologist at the wartime Mill Hill Emergency Hospital, he was appointed Professor of Psychology in the University of London, and Director of the Psychological Department at the Institute of Psychiatry (Maudsley & Bethlem Royal Hospitals). He has lectured in many countries, and has been Visiting Professor at the universities of Pennsylvania and California in the USA. Known mainly through his experimental research in the field of personality, he has written some five hundred articles in technical journals as well as several books including *Dimensions of personality* (1947), *The scientific study of personality* (1952), *The psychology of politics* (1954), *Experiments with drugs* (1963), *The uses and abuses of psychology* (1953), *Sense and nonsense in psychology* (1957), *Fact and fiction in psychology* (1969), *Know your own IQ* (1968), and *Crime and personality* (1977). He advocates the highest degree of scientific rigour in the design of psychological experiments and is very critical of much loose thinking at present under the guise of "psychology".

It is probably true to say that Hans Eysenck is the most famous living psychologist. He is notorious for his controversial work on such topics as race and IQ, smoking and cancer, and the psychology of politics. But he is famous for his work on personality theory and behaviour genetics which in many respects is now being recognized as being thirty years before its time. A scholarly, stable introvert he plays tennis every day and has been the subject of biographies, television programmes and many newspaper reports.

Some of the basic issues in psychology

Psychologists often disagree as to what psychology is, what methods should be used, and whether a theory is valid or not. Some of the issues they disagree on are very basic but others less so. Some are currently very controversial, others less important today. Together, however, they give a good idea of some of the major issues in psychology. Lundin (1985) has listed eight of these basic issues.

Mind versus body

This is the oldest and still one of the most important of the controversial issues in psychology today. It is usually stated as the mind–body problem. If one considers that in both man and animals there exists a body and a mind, several questions arise: How does one get from the body processes to the mental processes, presuming that they are separate entities? How are the mind and body related? Is there a connection, or are they completely separate? Is there a mind at all?

In psychology today, any system or theory which presumes both body *and* mind as part of psychology is called dualistic. Structuralism, the first psychological system to evolve, considered that both body and mind existed and if something happened physically, that was correlated with parallel mental events.

Earlier, the concept of mind was often identified with the theological notion of the soul or spiritual side of man. Many psychologists have maintained the dualistic tradition in one form or another. In more recent times, the earlier, simple terms of mind, consciousness, or mental life have taken on new terms such as ego (in Freudian psychology), cognitive maps, psychic energies, tension systems, psychic fields of force, stimulus trace, and so on. Although the more recent concepts are far more subtle, some kind of separation of the mental from the physical is accepted. The basic issue, then, is: should such dualistic concepts be encouraged as part of the study of psychology?

Subjectivism versus objectivism

This is closely related to the mind–body problem. An objective approach to psychology considers its data to be whatever can be seen or measured directly and precisely. To be objective is not necessarily synonymous with being experimental, although most experimental psychologists at least attempt to be as objective as they can in dealing with their data. Observation studies are objective. So are experiments where the researcher tries to manipulate the variables. However, if one were particularly interested in animal psychology, one might go out and *observe* various species in their natural habitat.

Subjectivism, on the other hand, refers to the more private inner and unobservable experiences a person has. He/she reports what he/she feels, thinks, or experiences. Since these events are a private matter for each individual, they cannot be shared except through words. They are not objectively observable. The side of the issue one cares to take depends on what one considers the study of psychology to be. If one considers matters of experiences and inner feelings to be important, then the subjective approach would be allowed. On the other hand, if one limits oneself to only observable behaviour, subjectivism must be denied. Of course it is possible to accept the validity of both sorts of data.

Quantification versus qualitative methods

The issue of quantification (measurement – how much?) versus qualification (evaluation – what sort of?) is often related to the objective–subjective issue. Subjective data are usually qualitative and cannot easily be quantified. A description of one's feelings can hardly be put into numbers. On the other hand, to quantify means some form of measurement must be taken. The measurement may be in terms of how often a particular response takes place (rate), of the amount of the response (magnitude), or of how long it takes for the response to occur (latency). In the case of rate, an example may be how many times a rat presses a bar in a given unit of time; in latency, how quickly one presses a button when a light is flashed on; in magnitude, how much saliva Pavlov's dogs secreted when the bell was rung.

The issue can also take the form of richness versus precision in terms of the data gathered. The clinical, or case-history, method in psychology is essentially qualitative, though it does not have to be exclusively so. It can be argued that this method is far richer in gathering facts and unearthing many crucial aspects about a person's life history.

Reductionism versus nonreductionism

The basic issue here involves whether or not the subject matter of psychology (however it may be defined) may stand on its own as independent of other sciences or should be reduced to a more basic level of analysis. The reductionists argue that the nonreductionists are merely describing and not explaining the basic causes of the psychological event, which they (the reductionists) feel must be found in internal physiological or other more fundamental functions. The nonreductionists, on the other hand, argue that psychology is an independent study with its own subject matter, which is just as legitimate as that of physiology, chemistry or physics and does not need to be reduced to a more basic level.

Molar versus molecular

This issue involves the kind of unit the psychologists ought to study. Should one study the whole (molar), or break it down into its separate component parts (molecular)? The question is whether one should study the reactions of the entire or whole organism (molar), or limit oneself to a description of simple discrete reflexes or responses (molecular). The Gestalt psychologists, who also stressed perception, rose up against the molecular approach, stating that it was impossible to break experiences down into elementary units. Psychology must deal with perception as a whole, and to break it down would destroy part of what one wished to study. They felt that the whole was not equal to the sum of its parts. A melody, for example, was more than the particular notes which made it up, and therefore must be perceived as a whole. Thus, as in other issues, we have considered the molar-molecular issue is a matter of opinion. Physiological psychologists tend to favour molecular approaches and social psychologists the molar approach.

Determinism versus free will

In order to have a deterministic view, one must presume that any behaviour is the result of the events that have happened earlier in the past history of the organism. The proponents of teleology, on the other hand, believe that the future (not the past) affects the present. Thus beliefs about what *will* occur, or future rewards, affect people's behaviour. Thus teleologists emphasize how expectations of what will or might happen determine current behaviour.

There is another side issue with regard to determinism: the notion of free will. According to those who accept free will, one's behaviour is not completely determined by past events, since man is capable of making his own decisions because he possesses the free will to do so. This will may or may not be dependent on past events. Humanistic psychologists take this position, because they believe that one of the aspects of being human is a capacity to make one's own decisions, not necessarily with regard to what has gone before. The determinists, on the other hand, maintain that any choice is a determined choice. The decision that is made results from the weight of past circumstances in one direction or the other.

Nativism versus empiricism, or heredity versus environment

This issue has deep philosophical roots, and can be stated in a number of ways. Among the earlier psychologies that stressed the study of experience and perception, the issue was how much of our experience came to us naturally in an inherent or unlearned fashion, as opposed to how much was the result of direct experience or observation. Descartes, in the seventeenth century, had stated that some ideas were inborn. But Locke asserted that all knowledge came from experience. Similarly, Kant stressed the importance of native or inborn perceptions of our world. In more contemporary psychology, the nativistic notion was adopted by the Gestalt psychologists who felt that certain ways in which we perceived our environment came to us quite naturally without the need for prior learning. For example, by the time human infants could crawl, they could naturally perceive depth and would not fall into a pit or over a cliff. The empirical tradition, in science and psychology in particular, has stressed the importance of gaining what we know from our direct observation of the facts and learning about them through our senses.

Also, in contemporary psychology, the issue takes another form, that of the nature–nurture or heredity–environment controversy. Here, the issue is stated in terms of learned versus unlearned behaviour. How much of our behaviour is dependent on hereditary factors such as native talents or capacities, as opposed to pure learning?

Today there is greater emphasis on instinctive behaviour (behaviour that is not learned but programmed in), particularly by those who study animals in their natural environments. Some psychologists feel that intelligence at the human level is based primarily on native or inherent endowment, depending on how effective the environment may be. Others, however, stress that intelligence is primarily a matter of experience and learning, provided that the person is not biologically damaged in some way. Earlier it was not uncommon to hear some people stating that certain races were either basically superior or inferior. However, on a more individual basis, the controversy is still very active about how much of a part heredity or environment play in the determination of our behaviour.

Theory versus data

Certain theories in psychology have been criticized as depending too much on theory and not enough on well-collected data. Freud did have a kind of data: his observations of what his patients told him as they lay on his couch. On the basis of these data, Freud constructed a very elaborate theory. His opponents criticized him not only for the unreliability of his data but for formulating constructs that seemed impossible to demonstrate – for example, the unconscious, psychic energy, libido, cathexes, and so-called punishments and rewards of the superego. Only a small part of Freud's position is based on solid data. What we are left with is largely theory.

At the other extreme are to be found psychologists who claim that theory is not necessary. They assert that all we need are the data, the results of an experiment. There is thus no need for theoretical propositions; the principles of psychology can be formulated from the data. Such a position was set forth by Skinner. He asserted that if an experiment is properly and precisely executed with all proper controls, the results stand for themselves and add to the principles of psychology.

Conclusion

Although it can trace its roots back to earlier centuries, psychology is really a twentieth-century science. It is only in this century, indeed the latter parts of it, that the profession of psychology has become fully established and accepted in the university world and beyond.

Despite its youth, psychology has developed distinct theoretical and methodological schools or approaches. This has occurred for different reasons; partly because of the influence of other academic disciplines like philosophy and zoology, but also because of the particular problems that the psychologists were studying. Animal and human behaviour are so diverse and complicated it is perhaps no wonder that very different methods and theories have developed to understand the processes being investigated.

Psychology, like all other disciplines, has had its fair share of early pioneers. American, British and German researchers' early work shaped many of the questions we are still concerned with today. But psychology has spread far and wide and universities on every continent have departments of psychology where researchers pursue scientific endeavours.

Like all other scientific disciplines there are different schools of thought in psychology. It is possible to characterize these in terms of abstract philosophic principles. Knowing about the past does help to explain why some topics were neglected while others studied then (like racial differences) have fallen into neglect. It also helps to understand where new movements and ideas in psychology fit into other more established fields of study.

Chapter 3

Major research methods in psychology

Psychologists study everything from memory in the octopus to schizophrenic breakdown in people. They study issues as diverse as learning, perception and social behaviour. As such they need a wide range of methods to investigate the issues that fascinate them. How psychologists go about their research is in itself interesting. They have to be imaginative and flexible because of the diversity of things they study and because if people are aware they are being studied their behaviour may not be typical.

The research process

Scientific knowledge is knowledge obtained by both reason and experience (observation). Logical validity and experimental verification are the criteria employed by scientists to evaluate claims for knowledge. These two criteria are translated into the research activities of scientists through the *research process*. The research process can be viewed as the overall scheme of scientific activities in which scientists engage in order to produce knowledge; it is the paradigm of scientific inquiry.

As illustrated in Figure 3.1, the research process consists of seven principal stages: *problem, hypothesis, research design, measurement, data collection, data analysis,* and *generalization*. Each of these stages is interrelated with *theory* in the sense that it is affected by it as well as affecting it. The most characteristic feature of the research process is its *cyclic nature*. It often starts with a problem and ends in a tentative generalization based on the experimental evidence. The generalization ending one cycle is the beginning of the next cycle. This cyclic process continues indefinitely, reflecting the progress of a scientific discipline.

The research process is also *self-correcting*. Tentative generalizations to research problems are tested logically and empirically. If these generalizations are rejected, new ones are formulated and tested. In the

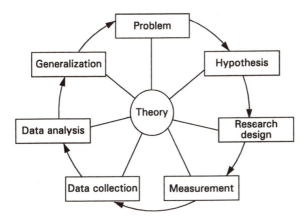

Figure 3.1 The principal stages of the research process.

process of formulation all research operations are re-evaluated because the rejection of a tentative generalization might be the result not of its being invalid, but of deficiencies in performing the research operations. To minimize the risk of rejecting true generalizations, one re-examines each of the stages in the research process prior to the formulation of new generalizations.

Psychology and all science is united by its methodology, but also by its subject matter. What sets the scientific approach apart from other modes of acquiring knowledge are the assumptions upon which it is grounded and its methodology.

The assumptions of the scientific approach are essentially these: behaviour is orderly; we can understand behaviour; knowledge is tentative but superior to ignorance; natural phenomena have natural causes; nothing is self-evident; knowledge is derived from the acquisition of experience.

The methodology of the scientific approach serves two major purposes: rules for communication; rules for logical and valid reasoning. These systems of rules allow us to understand, explain and predict our environments and ourselves in a manner that other systems for generating knowledge cannot allow us to do.

Scientific knowledge is knowledge provable by *both* reason and observation. The scientific methodology requires strict adherence to the rules of logic and observation. Such adherence should not be seen as encouraging conformity but rather as helping to know the correct use of the rules. Naturally psychologists, like other scientific communities, are involved in power struggles that are not always conducive to the progress of science. These struggles and fashions are inevitable. But claims for knowledge are accepted only in so far as they are congruent with the assumptions of science and its methodology.

Major methods of research

Psychological researchers are eclectic in their research methodology. A number of very different methods are available to the researcher to investigate psychological issues, test theories, or explore ideas. To some extent practical and ethical issues dictate which method is used, though often it is the preference and training of the researcher. Ideally, the research question should dictate which method is used and often this is the case. The following are some of the methods of research used in psychology. Each method has its advantages and disadvantages.

Psychology in the laboratory

Is it possible to measure behaviour in a lab? The psychology lab researcher's aim is to test the effects of one or more independent variables on one or more dependent variables. *Independent variables* in an experiment are those factors that are controlled or arranged by the experimenter and may often be considered the cause of behaviour. *Dependent variables* refer to those behaviours of the subject that are observed or recorded by the experimenter. Thus, if one is interested in whether television viewing encourages violence, the independent variable may be the amount and type of TV programmes watched and the dependent variable some measure of violent behaviour in the viewers.

Characteristic of the laboratory experiment is the investigator's ability to control the independent variables. Indeed, this aspect of control is one of the most important features of the laboratory experiment. Through this control, numerous extraneous variables could be eliminated, like light, noise, distraction, or other people present.

In addition to control, the laboratory experiment also offers another important advantage: the ability to assign subjects randomly to conditions. In order for investigators to draw conclusions regarding cause and effect, they must be sure that the pattern of results was not attributable to some systematic difference in the groups being compared. On average, *randomization* ensures an equality of subject characteristics across the various experimental conditions.

One other characteristic of the laboratory experiment should be mentioned: the *manipulation check.* Although experimenters are able to control the independent variables, it is still important for them to be sure that the subject in the experiment perceives the manipulation as it is intended. That is, if you want to include anxiety in subjects (by threatening them with a painful shock), you might measure their heart rate or ask them afterwards how scared they were.

Advantages

The advantages of the laboratory experiment as a means of acquiring knowledge have been largely summarized above. Principal among

these is the ability of the experimenter to control the independent variables and randomly to assign subjects to conditions. The two capabilities provide some basis for conclusions regarding cause and effect.
Furthermore, the laboratory allows the investigator to "sort out" factors – to simplify the more complex events of the natural world by
breaking them down into their component parts.

Disadvantages

Although the laboratory experiment has considerable advantages in
terms of its ability to isolate and control variables, it has substantial
disadvantages as well. In recent years, these disadvantages have
become the topic of considerable debate. Four of the major issues of
concern have been the possible irrelevance of the laboratory setting;
the reactions of subjects to the laboratory setting; the possible influence
of experimenters on their results; and deception and ethics.

The issue of relevance concerns the artificiality of the laboratory setting and the fact that many of the situations created in the laboratory
bear little direct relationship to the situations a person encounters in
real organizational life. One can distinguish between *experimental realism* and *mundane realism*: in the laboratory, one can devise situations
that have impact and that evoke valid psychological processes (experimental realism), even if the situation itself does not look like the real
world (mundane realism). Yet, it remains true that many laboratory
tasks seem suspiciously artificial and their *external validity* has not
been demonstrated. *External validity* refers to the "generalizability" of
research findings to the "outside world", to other populations, treatment variables and measurement variables.

A second criticism of the laboratory experiment focuses on the reactions of subjects to the laboratory setting. These reactions may involve
demand characteristics and *evaluation apprehension*. The first term refers to
the fact that the experimental setting may evoke certain demands. That
is, expectations on the part of subjects to act in the way that they think
the experimenter would wish. *Evaluation apprehension* refers to the concerns that a subject has about being observed and judged while in the
laboratory setting. Because subjects come to a laboratory experiment
knowing that the investigator is interested in some aspects of their
behaviour, they may try to present themselves in a favourable light.

A third criticism of the laboratory experiment concerns *experimenter
expectancies*. It has been shown in a variety of situations that an experimenter, knowing the hypothesis of the study, can unknowingly influence the results of the study.

The influence of these experimenter expectancies can be controlled
to a large extent. For example, many experiments involve instructions
that have been tape-recorded in advance, thus assuring constancy in
experimenter approach to all subjects. Other techniques include the

use of a "blind" experimenter, wherein the individual conducting the experiments is not informed of the experimental hypotheses and thus is less likely to exert a systematic bias on the results.

A fourth problem concerns the *ethics* of laboratory research, particularly when deception is involved. In order to ensure subjects are naïve about the point of the study (and to reduce demand characteristics and evaluation apprehension) they are often deceived; indeed, lied to about the study. Although they are fully debriefed afterwards the ethical problems must be faced.

Despite these well-understood problems the majority of psychological studies are done in laboratories, because the advantages are seen to outweigh the disadvantages!

Field experiments

In contrast to the laboratory experiment, the setting of the field experiment is a natural one and the subjects are not generally aware that they are subjects in an experiment. Rather than contriving an artificial situation in a laboratory, the investigator who uses a field experiment to test a hypothesis is looking at behaviour in its natural setting. For example, in order to study altruism (unselfish helping or pro-social behaviour) a psychologist may get an actor to collapse in the street or lie bottle-in-hand in the gutter while the experimenter observes the behaviour of passers-by.

Like the laboratory experiment, in the field experiment the experimenter has some control of the independent variables but rarely the random assignment of subjects to conditions.

Advantages

The advantages of the field experiment are that by focusing on behaviour in a natural setting, experimenters can be much more certain of the external validity of their findings. Furthermore, because subjects are generally unaware of their status as subjects, the problems of reactivity and the subjects' desire to be seen in a positive light are eliminated. In addition, because control over the independent variable and principles of randomization are maintained, the field experiment allows the same possibilities for conclusions about cause and effect as does the laboratory experiment.

Disadvantages

Although the field experiment may seem ideally to combine the application of the strict rules of experimentation with the realism of natural behaviour settings, it too has some disadvantages. These disadvantages relate to the nature of the independent variable, the nature of the dependent variable, the ethics of the experiment and the practical difficulties involved.

Because the experimenter is working in a complex natural setting where many events may be occurring simultaneously, the independent variable in the study must be obvious to the potential subject. Subtle manipulations of a variable may simply go unnoticed. The experimental independent variable is, in effect, competing with all of the other stimuli present in the setting.

The dependent variable in a field experiment needs to be selected carefully. The experimenters must be able to readily observe and reliably judge the dependent-variable behaviour. An additional problem in field experimentation concerns ethics. Is it reasonable for the investigator to involve individuals in an experiment without their knowledge or permission? Finally, the field experiment often poses practical problems. In contrast to the investigator in the laboratory, the investigator in the field has no control over the majority of events in the environment; unexpected events may reduce or destroy the effectiveness of the manipulation.

Quasi-experimental research

The defining characteristics of quasi-experimental research are that the investigator does not have full experimental control over the independent variables but does have extensive control over how, when and for whom the dependent variable is measured (Rosnow & Rosenthal 1992). Generally, these experiments involve behaviour in a natural setting and focus on the effect of intervention in a system of ongoing behaviour. For instance, imagine the television stations in a particular part of the country go on strike. This allows one the perfect and rare opportunity to see what people do when deprived of the "box" compared to those who are not.

In other cases, the intervention may be a natural disaster, such as floods, an earthquake or a tornado. Power blackouts could serve as the independent variable in a study of reactions to stressful events; or the introduction of new laws. The experimenter would have no control over the independent variable, but could carefully select a set of dependent variables to measure the effect of the phenomena. Consider whether TV advertisements trying to stop drink–driving work: if one region runs ads of this sort and the other doesn't (perhaps because of cost), one can see what effect they have by measuring actual drink-related behaviour after the series of advertisements and comparing the two regions.

Advantages

One unique advantage of quasi-experimental research conducted in a natural setting is that it allows for the study of very strong variables that cannot be manipulated or controlled by the experimenter. Often, too, quasi-experimental research deals with policy decisions that have consequences for very large numbers of people. The broad impact of such decisions gives considerable weight to the external validity of the study, in a manner that can rarely be matched in the more limited laboratory or field experiment.

Disadvantages

Because the investigator has no control over the primary independent variable in quasi-experimental research, it is always possible that other uncontrolled variables are affecting the dependent-variable behaviour. Random assignment of subjects to conditions can rarely be assumed in the quasi-experimental design, either. Often such research must literally be done "on the run". Furthermore, the arbitrariness of events in the quasi-experimental world precludes the experimenter's ability to vary factors according to any theoretical model. Intensity of a stressful event, for example, might be an important variable in predicting the nature of response to stress. Nonetheless, it is clearly impossible for the experimenter to control such a variable, and hence the levels of intensity would need to be accepted as they naturally occurred.

Field study

Most field studies are characterized by their in-depth consideration of a limited group of people. The investigator in this setting plays a more reactive role than in the field experiment. Rather than manipulate some aspect of the environment and observe the changes that occur, the investigator in the field study records as much information as possible about the characteristics of that situation without altering the situation in any substantial way. Most often, people in the environment are aware of the investigator's presence and the general purpose of the investigation. Many times the investigator is a *participant observer* – that is, someone actively engaged in the activities of the group while at the same time maintaining records of the group members' behaviours.

Observation is the key element of the field study method. Considerable time must be devoted in advance to familiarizing oneself with the environment and becoming aware of the kinds of behaviours that are most likely to occur. Then, one must decide which types of behaviour are to be recorded.

Once categories of behaviour are selected for observation, the investigator must devise specific methods of recording the desired information. Finally, the observer must conduct a series of preliminary investigations to *determine the reliability* of the measures. In other words, it must be demonstrated that a series of different observers watching the same event and using the methods chosen to record observations will code the behaviour in the same way. Despite such reliability, a coding system merely reflects one observer's biases and cannot be used as a basis for scientific statements.

Advantages

The major advantage lies in its realism. The focus of the study is on events as they normally occur in a real-life setting. Furthermore, because most field studies take place over an extended period of time, they provide information about the sequence and development of behaviours that cannot be gained in the one-shot observation typical of field and laboratory experiments. Additionally, the duration of the field study generally allows for the collection of several different types of dependent measures.

Disadvantages

Well-conducted field studies furnish a wealth of data, but the lack of control in such settings can be a problem. Because there is no controlled independent variable, it is difficult to form conclusions regarding cause and effect. Although there are some statistical techniques to assist in making causal conclusions, the process is a more difficult one than in the controlled experimental design. A second potential problem in the field study is the subject's awareness of the investigator's observations. When subjects are aware of being observed, their behaviour may be reactive – that is, influenced by the process of observation. Most experienced observers believe, however, that in a long-term field study the subjects become indifferent to the observer's presence, although the problem remains a serious one in briefer studies.

Archival research

Archival research refers to the analysis of any existing records that have been produced or maintained by persons or organizations other than the experimenter. In other words, the original reason for collecting the records was not a psychological experiment. Newspaper reports and government records of airplane fatalities are two examples of archival data. Other sources of material include books and magazines, folk stories of preliterate societies, personal letters and speeches by public figures.

Advantages

First, it allows the investigator to test hypotheses over a wider range of time and societies than would otherwise be possible. Many records date back for centuries, a *period of time that cannot be examined today using the other methods we have discussed.* Demonstrating the validity of a hypothesis in a number of different cultures and historical periods, instead of being restricted to a specific group in the present time and place, gives us *considerable confidence in the validity of that hypothesis* as a test of human behaviour in general.

A second advantage of the archival method is that it uses *unobtrusive measures*: it did not cause reactivity in the participants at the time the data were collected. Because the information used in archival research was originally collected for some other purpose, there is little or no chance that demand characteristics or evaluation apprehension will be problems for the present investigator.

Disadvantages

Although experimenters doing research did not collect the data personally and thus are spared some problems in terms of reactivity, they may encounter some difficulties in terms of data availability. Frequently a researcher will not be able to locate the kind of data needed to test a hypothesis. Not being able to design the dependent measures, the investigator is left at the mercy of those who collected the data. Sometimes, of course, creativity and ingenuity will help the investigator to locate the kinds of data needed; in other cases, however, missing or inaccurate records will prevent an adequate experimental test. Even if the material is available, it is sometimes difficult to categorize it in the way necessary to answer the research question. Such procedures are time consuming, although the development of computer programs has provided a welcome assistance in some instances.

Simulation and role playing

Although the range of simulation studies is considerable, the aim of each is to imitate some aspect of a real-world situation in order to gain more understanding of people's psychological processes. Subjects in these studies are typically asked to *role play*: to adopt a part and act as if they were in the real situation. In advance of their participation, the subjects are fully informed about the situation and are asked to develop their part to the best of their ability.

Advantages

The success of simulation or role-play study depends heavily on the degree of involvement that the experimental setting can engender. If the subjects get deeply involved in the setting, then the simulation may well approximate the real-life conditions that it intends to match. Furthermore, because participants are fully informed of the purposes of the study in advance, they basically take on the role of co-investigators, a role that is both ethically and humanistically more satisfying in many respects than the more typical experimental subject role in which the subject is unaware of many of the experimenter's intentions. An additional advantage of the simulation is that it may allow the investigator to study, in the laboratory, phenomena and situations that are difficult to study in the real world.

Disadvantages
In spite of their advantages, simulation and role playing are two of the most controversial methods in the social psychological repertoire. Critics of the method claim that when one asks subjects to act as if they are in a certain role, the subjects will do only what they think they *might* do and not necessarily what they *would* do in the real situation (Nachmias & Nachmias 1981).

In addition, the problems of experimental demands and evaluation apprehension, discussed earlier in relation to laboratory experiments, are even more serious when the subject is fully informed of the purposes of the study. On the other hand, proponents of role playing argue that, to some degree, the participant in an experiment is always playing a role, whether it is the general role of subject or a more specific role defined by the investigator.

Surveys and interviews
While many other methods in psychology make use of questionnaires as *part* of their procedures, survey and interview methods rely *solely* on this type of information. In both cases, the investigator defines an area for research and designs a set of questions that will elicit the beliefs, attitudes and self-reported experiences of the respondent in relation to the research topic.

Designing a good questionnaire is not as simple as it may appear! Some considerations that enter into the design include the wording of questions, the provision of sufficient responses and the format of the questionnaire itself. Considerable pretesting is necessary to ensure that the questions are objective, unbiased, understandable to the average respondent and specific enough to elicit the desired information.

When the questionnaire is being presented by an interviewer, additional precautions against biasing the responses are necessary. The issue of experimenter bias, discussed earlier in relation to laboratory experiments, can be a problem in the interview method if the interviewer consciously or unconsciously encourages some responses and discourages or seems uninterested in others. Thus, interviewers must be carefully trained to standardize the delivery of questions to respondents. In addition, the interview method requires some skills on the part of the interviewer in developing a rapport, so that the respondent will be willing to answer questions in a straightforward and honest manner. Interviews are notoriously unreliable if not conducted by highly trained personnel.

In both questionnaire surveys and interviews, the investigator must be concerned with *sampling procedures.* That is, who should be asked to complete the questionnaire so that one can get a representative picture.

Advantages

A major advantage of both survey questionnaires and interviews is that they allow the investigator to formulate the issues of concern very specifically. Rather than devising a situation to elicit desired behaviour or finding a natural situation in which to observe that behaviour, constructors of questionnaires directly question people about the behaviour or area under investigation. Survey questionnaires are easier and more economical to use than interview procedures. In addition, they provide a greater anonymity for the respondent, which is important in the case of sensitive or personal issues. Face-to-face interviews, on the other hand, allow the interviewer to gather additional information from observation. Furthermore, the interviewer can clarify questions that may be confusing to the respondent and assure that the person intended to answer the questions is indeed the person responding.

Disadvantages

Perhaps the major difficulty with self-report data, whether from interviews or surveys, is the issue of accuracy. Some questions may lead to embellishments by the respondent, who attempts to appear in a favourable light. As suggested earlier, survey questionnaires and interviews also have opposite sets of weaknesses. The survey questionnaire gives the investigator less control over the situation and cannot assure the conditions under which the questionnaire is being administered, who is answering it and whether the respondent fully understands the questions. For its part, the interview is more costly, more time consuming and is more susceptible to examiner bias. In summary, questionnaire and interview methods allow the investigator to ask directly about the issues of concern. Particularly in the case of questionnaires, very-large-scale studies are possible, thus allowing greater generalizability of the results. Both methods, however, rely on the accuracy and honesty of the respondent and depend on self-reports of behaviour rather than observations of the behaviour itself.

Tests

Over the years, psychologists have constructed a huge number of tests to measure such things as personality, ability, vocational preferences, art appreciation. Some of the best-known tests are those measuring intelligence and those measuring personality. Tests can be used as either an independent or a dependent variable. As an independent variable one can see whether tests predict different types of behaviour

– i.e. do IQ tests predict A-level results – or one may be interested in how training courses affect test scores. They are widely used and equally widely criticized.

Advantages

These include the fact that tests provide numeric information, which means that individuals can be more easily compared on the same criteria. In interviews, different questions are asked of different candidates, and the answers often forgotten. Tests provide comparable profiles. Also with data-based records, one can trace a person's development over time. In fact, by going back to test results kept in a person's file one can actually see if, and by how much, the tests were predictive of occupational success. Tests give explicit and specific results on temperament and ability rather than vague, ambiguous, coded platitudes that are so often found in references. A percentage or a test score (provided of course that it is valid) makes for much clearer thinking about personal characteristics than terms like "satisfactory", "sufficient" or "high-flyer". Good norms demonstrate a candidate's scores relative to the population so that people know how they match up.

Tests, it is argued, are fairer because they eliminate corruption and favouritism, and prevent old-boy, Mason – or Oxbridge – networks from self-perpetuating. That is, if a person does not have the ability or has a "dangerous' profile", they will not be chosen irrespective of their other "assets". Moreover, tests are comprehensive in that they cover all of the basic dimensions of personality and ability from which other occupational behaviour patterns derive. A good test battery can give a complete picture of individual functioning.

It has also been suggested that most psychological tests are scientific in that they are soundly empirically based on proven theoretical foundations – that is, they are reliable, valid and able to discriminate the good from the mediocre and the average from the bad. Tests also increase the psychological concepts and language of those that use them. This gives those who are not trained in personality theory a very useful set of concepts that they can use to identify and distinguish human characteristics in the workplace.

Practical data resulting from the tests can be used to settle practical arguments. That is, objective numbers provide the sort of clear evidence to justify decisions. Finally, tests give testers and testees alike interesting and powerful insights into their own beliefs and behaviours. They might also be used to explain to candidates why they have been rejected.

Disadvantages

An obvious and common complaint is that these tests are fakeable – that is, people like to describe themselves in a positive light and receive a "desirable" score so that they may be accepted. Yet this faking in a way reflects their "real" personality. Some tests have lie scores to attempt to overcome this. The effects of this distortion are, however, not major. And, of course, this problem does not apply to tests of ability or intelligence!

Some people do not have sufficient self-insight to report on their own feelings and behaviour – that is, it is not that people lie but they cannot, rather than will not, give accurate answers about themselves (some tests only look for simple behavioural data to overcome this).

Tests are sometimes dismissed as unreliable in that all sorts of temporary factors – test anxiety, boredom, weariness, a headache, period pains – lead people to give different answers on different occasions. Although this is partly true, this factor only makes a small difference. Most importantly, tests may be invalid – they do not measure what they say they are measuring and these scores do not predict behaviour over time. For many tests, this is indeed the Achilles heel and they are lamentably short of robust proof of their validity. It is supremely important that tests have a predictive validity: scores predict behaviour accurately.

Some people point out that tests might be able to measure all sorts of dimensions of behaviour but not the ones crucial to the organization, like trustworthiness and likelihood of absenteeism. Buying personality tests is like having a set menu, but what many managers want is an *à la carte* menu from which they can select only what they want.

It is also true that people have to be sufficiently literate or articulate to do these tests, not to mention sufficiently familiar with North American jargon. Many organizations therefore believe that their workforce could not do them properly, and that they would take up too much time or would cause needless embarrassment. Another relevant criticism is that there are no good norms, at least not for the populations they want to test, and comparing them to American students (Caucasian sophomores) is dangerously misleading (this is certainly true, but not in all instances). Hence it is frequently argued that many psychological tests are unfair and biased in favour of White Anglo-Saxon Protestants (WASPS), so that white males tend to do better or get a more attractive profile – and therefore get selected – than say black females. They therefore fly in the face of antidiscriminatory legislation.

Also, freedom of information legislation may mean that candidates themselves would be able to see and hence challenge the scores, their interpretation and the decision made based on them. The less objective the recorded data, the better for those unprepared to give negative feedback.

As (ability and personality) tests become well known, people could buy copies and practise so that they know the correct or most desirable answers. This happens extensively with General Measure Aptitude

Tests (GMATs), and results could be seen to be linked more with preparation and practice than actual ability.

Unobtrusive measures

Many of the methods of collecting data outlined above are reactive – the self-consciousness of the subjects may affect the nature of the results. People may be guilty, embarrassed, clumsy or simply nervous being questioned or watched; hence psychologists have tried what are called unobtrusive measures. One of the most famous is the lost-letter technique where psychologists "lose" a letter, perhaps addressed to a local or a foreign person, and count whether prejudice is manifest by the finder's "helpfully" posting it or ripping it up. Some psychologists have even advocated "garbology". That is, going through people's rubbish to find out what they have thrown away (e.g. empty alcohol bottles, etc.) Responses to advertisements of different kinds have also been examined.

Critics point out that these measures are rarely very reliable. They also note some of the ethical problems in fooling people. And of course there are no control factors so one cannot be certain what chance events are affecting the behaviour examined.

Advantages

The major advantage of using unobtrusive measures is that they are usually free of the self-conscious manipulation of obtrusive measures. Take the drinking of alcohol: most people underestimate how much they drink and very heavy drinkers may strenuously deny the extent of their drinking. But actually counting their discarded bottles gives one a very real indication of the extent of their habit.

Disadvantages

The primary disadvantage of the use of unobtrusive measures – like measuring the wear on the tyres of a disabled person's wheelchair to measure the person's mobility – is that one cannot be absolutely sure of underlying causes. In other words, all sorts of other factors that you may not know about may have affected the thing that you are measuring.

Conclusion

The range of research methods used by psychologists gives one a good idea of the variety of problems they investigate and the way they do this. Experimental psychologists often use laboratory-based studies; social psychologists frequently use questionnaires. Developmental and animal psychologists frequently use detailed observation techniques.

No one method is correct, but given the balance of advantages and disadvantages, it does seem the case that certain psychological processes are best measured by some approaches rather than others.

Psychology like all sciences is changing and thus new methods are being developed, or old methods rediscovered. There is, for instance, a renewed interest among social psychologists in qualitative methods such as group discussions, focus groups and in-depth interviews. The material that emerges (recorded and then transcribed on to paper) is subjected to various forms of analysis, such as discourse analysis, which attempts to discover the theories, ideas and motives behind the speakers involved.

Some methodologies move in and out of fashion but others remain quite constant in terms of their use and popularity. It remains true that often the nature of the problem dictates the research method used, although the beliefs of the experimenter are also pretty important in determining which of the different methods is chosen.

Chapter 4
What goes on in psychology?

By this stage we hope we have given you some idea of what in general psychology is, how it developed as a science and some of the methods which may be employed in researching psychological issues. But what do psychologists actually do? In particular, what do psychology students do, what do researchers in psychology do and what do the increasing band of people who have chosen to make psychology their career do? We will look at the first two of these questions in this chapter and consider the question of what psychology can be used for and by whom in Chapter 5. The final chapter is a guide on how to start on the road to becoming a psychologist yourself, or at least a fully-fledged student of psychology, should you wish to consider following that route.

Psychology in schools, colleges and universities

One way of discovering what a student in psychology might be taught at school, college or university is to take a look at a general textbook in psychology, such as one of those listed in Chapter 6. A typical list of textbook contents is as follows. Each of the areas receives approximately equal consideration.

- *The nature of psychology*. This section would be expected to include an exploration of psychology as a science, its history and the major issues it addresses.
- *Methods of psychological research*. Reviews the major approaches to research and varieties of research methods, including how to design experiments and an introduction to the use of statistics in psychology.
- *Biological processes*. Without a brain, a nervous system and the body they serve there would be no psychology! So psychologists learn about nerve cells and the way they work, about hormones

and how the brain is constructed. This section might also consider how nervous systems change through maturation or through experience and the importance of heredity and our evolutionary history in making us what we are today.

- *Sensation and perception.* Considers how our bodies detect light, sound, odour and touch and how our brains convert these raw sensations into perceptions; that is, our experience of things we can see, hear, smell, feel and interact with, of size and shape, of depth and colour. Sometimes this conversion process goes awry and what we perceive is an illusion.
- *Consciousness and altered mental states.* Explores how and why our mental experience varies during sleep and dreaming, in hypnosis or when we meditate or take drugs of various sorts.
- *Learning and conditioning.* Deals with the varieties of learning in humans and animals and the principles which underlie behaviour.
- *Memory.* Considers different types of memory, such as working memory, short-term and long-term memory, and the effects of brain injuries on memory. An increasingly important topic is memory, and its shortcomings, in everyday situations.
- *Language and thought.* Explores the mechanisms of thinking, reasoning, decision making and problem solving. The development, use and understanding of language and the relationship between thought and language are other central issues.
- *Psychological development.* Describes stages of development in physical abilities and mental processes from birth (or even before), through childhood, adolescence and into adulthood. Particularly important topics are the development of language, of a sense of self and of moral reasoning as well as the contribution of experience versus inbuilt factors to these developments.
- *Motivation.* Why do we do things? What moves us to action? Among the answers on offer are hunger, thirst, sex, curiosity and the need to achieve. Again the question arises, are we born with these motives, or do we acquire them?
- *Emotion.* How is an emotional experience produced – in our bodies or in our minds? Other concerns are the ways in which emotion is expressed through facial expressions and body language, the effects of emotion on memory and judgement. Aggression is often the emotion most heavily featured.
- *Mental abilities and their measurement.* Describes the design and use of tests and measures in psychology. Key problems discussed include the nature of intelligence and, possibly, the role of heredity.
- *Personality and individual differences.* Our unique personality is what distinguishes us from others. The question of how personality is formed and developed is often presented in textbooks by contrasting major theories, such as the psychoanalytic or social-

learning approaches.
- *Abnormal psychology.* Looks at the various ways in which our psychological adjustment and mental health can break down. It ranges from the commonplace problems of anxiety and stress, and how we cope with them, to less common conditions such as phobias (abnormal fears), eating disorders (anorexia and bulimia), depression and schizophrenia.
- *Psychological therapies.* A wide variety of approaches to treating psychological disorders are described, contrasted and evaluated – from psychodynamic therapy, based on Freud's theories, to the more recent behavioural and cognitive therapies.
- *Social psychology and interpersonal relations.* Much to the annoyance of social psychologists this topic is commonly treated last in psychology textbooks. It covers a wide range of issues, such as the way we understand our own behaviour and that of others, how our attitudes are formed and change, why we are attracted to some people and not others, why we conform to social pressures, why we sometimes help our fellow humans and why we sometimes ignore or even harm them. Gender issues would have been raised in many of the earlier sections but have become a particular focus for some social psychologists in recent years.

Cognitive science

One development in psychology which the potential student should know about is the emergence of cognitive science as an identifiable field of study. Cognitive science is the science of the mind. It is concerned with those parts of psychology which focus on "cognitive processes" (literally mental processes related to "knowing"), such as perceiving, remembering, reasoning, decision making and problem solving. It is concerned with the way information is processed and represented in human brains and human minds in order to bring about these cognitive capabilities and the intelligent behaviour which depends on them. It seeks to understand and to model the fundamental properties of the brain and mind that make it possible for humans to see, think and feel, and to communicate. The possibility that the same, or similar, mental processes can be simulated by inanimate information-processing systems such as computers has generated a powerful new subject closely associated with cognitive science, that of "artificial intelligence". Most importantly, however, cognitive science extends beyond the boundaries of psychology to include other disciplines such as anthropology, philosophy, neuroscience, linguistics and computer science. Cognitive science is not usually treated separately in schools or colleges, but one possibility at university level is to study cognitive science alongside psychology or one of the other related disciplines.

The structure of a university degree course in psychology

A direct way of discovering what a university degree course in psychology might entail would be to take a look at a departmental timetable. A common format for the degree course is for it to extend over a three-year period, with the students having relatively little say in what they study in the first two years but with a wide choice of topics in the third year.

As an example, the list of courses offered by one large psychology department is given below. Where courses with the same, or similar, name appear in more than one year the content is different and more advanced in the later year(s). In all cases, the courses in any one year are roughly equal in weighting so far as teaching time and their contribution to the overall examination mark are concerned. For this particular department the courses taken in the third year count more towards the final degree mark than those from the first two years.

Year one
- Biological aspects of behaviour
- Developmental psychology
- General introduction to human experimental psychology (perception, attention, memory, learning, skills, speech, etc.)
- Introduction to psychological experimentation*
- Introduction to statistical methods in psychology
- Social psychology and individual differences

Year two
- Computing for psychologists (optional)
- Design and analysis of psychological experiments and abnormal psychological processes
- Language, cognition and memory
- Perception, information processing and skills
- Psychobiology and learning
- Research and quantitative methods in psychology*
- Social interaction

* These two courses are largely laboratory based and involve spending approximately one day per week during term time planning, carrying out and analyzing a series of small experimental studies.

Year three
Students select six of the following courses, with some restraints to ensure a balanced course:
- Advanced multivariate statistical methods in psychology
- Atypical (abnormal) development
- Cognitive and social development
- Development of cognitive systems

- Hearing
- Human neuropsychology
- Language and cognition
- Learning and motivation
- Mathematical and computational psychology
- Memory
- Movement and skills
- Neurobiology of vision
- Occupational psychology and ergonomics
- Personality and psychopathology (abnormal psychology)
- Philosophical issues in psychology
- Psychology of education
- Social psychology
- Speech
- Theories of mind and knowledge
- Visual perception

In addition, in the third year students carry out individual research projects on a topic of their own choosing, with a member of the academic staff acting as their personal supervisor. The project carries equivalent weight to two third-year courses (i.e. one-quarter of the whole year) in terms of time spent and marks allocated. Topics chosen for the project may range over areas as diverse as from hypnosis and pain to social learning in rats; from risk-taking behaviour to moral reasoning in children; from the psychology of money to the control of stuttering; from face perception to computer modelling; from the social psychology of sport to memory for everyday events; from handedness in mentally retarded children to psychological effects of breast cancer; from Soviet psychology to memory for odours; from perceptions of female/male sexuality to eating disorders; from stress and dizziness to children's memory for conversations; from separation anxiety in 4-year-olds to the psychological needs of those who care for the elderly.

You will find that course content and structure vary slightly across psychology departments and that some will, for instance, offer psychology related work-experience as part of the course. However, the above gives some idea of the range of topics covered and the relative importance which is attached to them.

Examples of research in psychology

Psychology, as we have said, is a very *diverse* discipline. One way of highlighting that diversity, as well as addressing the question of what psychologists do when they carry out research, is to review some of the more famous, and some not-so-famous, pieces of research from different areas of psychology. That is what we will do in the following sections. In such a short review we will inevitably rely quite heavily on the older, "classic" experiments, although we do feature some more recent work as well. There is so much new and exciting research taking place that it is impossible to do it justice here. It is there for you to discover for yourself as you read further into the subject.

You will find most of the topics listed in the previous section of this chapter represented in this brief review and it may be useful for you to try to decide which area any given experiment represents. One thing you may discover is that many topics do not seem to fit neatly into the textbook categories but seem to spill over into other areas. This is as it should be. Psychology is not only a diverse science, it is an *integrated* science in which explanations of human behaviour are sought by drawing together strands of evidence from a wide variety of sources.

Mental balancing acts, deceit and fried grasshoppers

An influential idea in psychology has been that people will try to maintain clear logical relationships (or balance) between the cognitions (knowledge, thoughts and ideas) they have about themselves, their actions and about the world in general. A consequence of this is that an individual whose cognitions are not consistent will experience mental discomfort and will strive consciously or unconsciously to achieve a mental balance in various ways. This unbalanced state is usually referred to as one of "cognitive dissonance". An example of unbalanced cognitions might be:

A. "Smoking causes cancer" and B. "I smoke cigarettes".

Believing A is not really consistent with the behaviour underlying B. Clearly, the individual harbouring these two ideas might achieve balance by *either* changing belief A to something like "The evidence that smoking causes cancer is not very strong – my father smoked all his life and lived until he was 90", *or* by stopping the behaviour underlying B to allow it to change to "I no longer smoke cigarettes". There is, however, a third possible way our smoker can escape the discomfort of mental imbalance and that is by adding a sort of mental counterweight in the form of a third cognition (C) which acts as a balancer or "justifier". In our example this could be achieved as follows:

A. "Smoking causes cancer" and B. "I smoke cigarettes" *but* C. "I need to smoke to calm down – without cigarettes life wouldn't be worth living".

Research has shown that if the justifier (C) is sufficiently large, mental balance is achieved and cognitions A and B can remain unchanged. If, however, conditions are set up so that the justifier is too small, then changes occur in either cognitions A or B to complete the balancing act, sometimes in surprising ways.

The classic example of this was provided by Festinger and Carlsmith (1959). In their experiment, subjects endured an hour of a tedious task such as repeatedly turning the pegs in a pegboard one-quarter to the right and then one-quarter to the left. They were then asked to tell the next "subject" (who was really an accomplice of the experimenter) that the experiment was interesting and that they had enjoyed taking part in it. One group of subjects received 20 dollars for doing this and another group received one dollar. All the real subjects in the experiment were then asked "in confidence" to say how interesting they had in fact found the experiment – "for the Psychology Department's own records". A control group who had carried out the task but had not been told to tell anyone it was interesting rated the task, as expected, as "dull and boring". The same was true of the group who had received 20 dollars for telling the next "subject" it was interesting. The group who had received only one dollar for this deceit, however, when asked for their honest opinion later rated the experiment as "fairly interesting". At first sight it is perhaps surprising that the group who received only one dollar should have found the experiment more enjoyable than those who received 20 dollars. The explanation is easy to see, however, if we consider the cognitions held by the 1-dollar and the 20-dollar groups. For both of them initially they were along the following lines:

A. "The task was dull and boring" and B. "I told someone that it was interesting".

For the 20-dollar group, a third cognition (C) – "I was paid a large amount to say the experiment was interesting" – acts as an effective balancer or justifier and so no change in cognitions A and B is necessary. For the 1-dollar group, however, the corresponding cognition C – "I was paid a small amount to say the experiment was interesting" – was an insufficient counterweight to achieve mental balance and so cognition A changed enough to be balanced by cognition C (in this case it is very difficult to change cognition B as this relates to a publicly committed act). The 1-dollar subjects thus ended up with a balanced set of cognitions:

A. "The task was fairly interesting", B. "I told someone that it was interesting" and C. "I was paid a little to say it was interesting".

Thus an apparently genuine change in the subjects' beliefs in the intrinsically interesting nature of the task had occurred in the course of this particular mental balancing act.

Assuming that most people express an initial dislike of the idea of eating fried grasshoppers, you might like to use the idea of mental balance to predict whether people who eat this particular delicacy for the first time at the request of a pleasant, friendly experimenter enjoy the experience more or less than people who do the same at the request of an unpleasant experimenter. An experiment of this sort was reported by Smith (1961) and the result is given at the end of this chapter.

Conformity and compliance: only obeying orders

Because it has important social and political implications, social psychologists have always been concerned with the question of how the presence of other people influences the actions of individuals. In particular, to what extent individuals will change their own behaviour to meet the explicit or implicit demands of the social situation in which they find themselves. One strand of this research concerns the extent to which individuals will conform to the apparent pressures of the group. A classic experiment on conformity was carried out by Asch (1956). A subject was seated in a room with 6–8 other people. The task they were to carry out was a very simple one of saying which of three comparison lines was the same length as a standard line. The task was set to be so easy that subjects normally never failed to recognize the correct line (see Fig. 4.1). The other people in the room were in fact accomplices of the experimenter and they sat in a row with the real subject sitting next to the end. They were asked to call out their answers in order going along the row. Most of the time everyone called out the same correct answer as to which of the comparison lines matched the standard line. On certain predetermined trials, however, the accomplices consistently gave the same wrong answer. Seventy-five per cent of the genuine subjects in experiments of this sort were swayed by the majority and gave the same (wrong) answer on at least one of these critical trials, some subjects on all of them. When questioned afterwards, very few of the subjects claimed to have seen the stimuli as the accomplices appeared to have seen them on critical trials but many were led to doubt their own perceptual abilities or their understanding of the experiment. They made comments such as "I thought that maybe because I wore glasses there was some defect" or "At first I thought I had the wrong instructions and then that there was something wrong with my eyes and my head". Whatever their private beliefs, a large number of subjects in a situation like this seem prepared to conform by giving answers which correspond to those of the rest of the group.

When the number of accomplices in the group is varied, conformity on the part of the subject seems to increase as the group size increases to three or four but then stabilizes or even decreases. The latter appears to be because the real subject begins to become suspicious that, for so

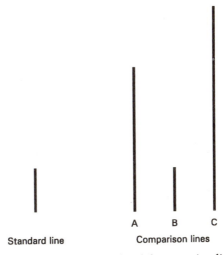

A   B   C
Standard line   Comparison lines

Figure 4.1 An example of the test stimuli used by Asch (1956) in his conformity tests.

many people all to give what seems like an erroneous response, there must be some sort of conspiracy or that all the others are blindly following what the first person says (Insko et al. 1985). Other research has shown that people who are anxious and seek approval from others are more likely to conform in this type of situation and that women are more likely to conform than men if they are being watched by others, although these effects are relatively weak ones and depend on the situation in which testing is carried out (Eagly & Chrvala 1986).

The degree to which subjects conform in experiments similar to those of Asch depends to some extent on the number of other people in the group, their status, how consistent they are in their answers, and so forth, as well as on the personal characteristics of the subject. We might also feel that if the consequences of our actions were more serious than in Asch's experiment we would be able to resist the pressure to conform, even if that pressure came from an apparently authoritative source. Would you for instance follow an order to apply potentially lethal shocks to a totally innocent victim?

When he was accused of killing over 100 defenceless Vietnamese villagers, Lieutenant Calley argued that he was merely following orders. Those were times of war and soldiers were under great pressure and stress. But what would happen in a quiet part of New Haven, Connecticut? An experiment to discover just this was reported by Milgram (1963). He had recruited 40 ordinary American men of different ages and occupations to take part in an experiment for a fee. They were told that the purpose of the study was to determine the effects of punishment on learning. They drew lots for the role of teacher and learner but unknown to them the draw was rigged so that the real subjects would always be the teacher and an accomplice of the experimenter would always be the learner. The experimenter was present throughout the experiment.

First of all, the "teacher" watched as the "learner" was strapped into a chair and electrodes were attached to his wrist. The volunteer teacher, now in an adjacent room, read a series of word pairs (Blue – Box, Wild – Duck, etc.) to the learner and then read the first word of the pair along with four other words. The learner's job was to indicate which of the four words was part of the original pair by pressing a switch that lit a light in the teacher's room. The teacher was told to administer a shock to the learner each time a wrong response was given, using a shock generator with 30 separate switches which increased by 15-volt increments from 15 to 450 volts. These were labelled from "Slight shock" at the low end to "Danger: severe shock" and finally "XXX" at the top end. This equipment was fake and the learner (who you will recall was the experimenter's accomplice) never actually received a shock, but the appearance of the whole set-up was highly convincing. After each wrong answer (of which the learner made many), the experimenter instructed the teacher (the real subject) to move one level higher on the shock generator. As the higher levels of shock were reached, the teacher could hear the shouts and protests of the learner. When the teacher reached 300 volts, the learner began to pound on the wall between the two rooms, and from then on was ominously silent in response to the questions posed by the teacher. At this point, the teacher usually turned to the experimenter for guidance. In a firm and rather stern voice, the experimenter replied that no answer was to be treated as a wrong answer and the learner was to be shocked according to the proper schedule. What the experimenter was interested in was how many subjects would continue to administer shocks to the end of the series, following his orders. Of the 40 volunteers, 26 (65 per cent) continued to the end of the shock series, and not a single person stopped prior to administering 300 volts, the point at which the learner began pounding on the wall. The experimenter concluded that obedience to commands is a strong force in our society, since nearly two-thirds of his volunteers obeyed his instructions even though they were led to believe they were seriously hurting another human being. In some instances a 450-volt shock could kill a person!

The work of Asch and Milgram led to the famous prison experiment carried out at Stanford University by Zimbardo and his colleagues (Haney et al. 1978). In this experiment ordinary students were assigned the roles of either inmates or guards in a simulated prison situation. The experiment was intended to run for two weeks but had to be stopped after six days because the behaviour of the student guards had become cruel, punitive and coercive. Equally, the students who were the "prisoners" were showing abnormal behaviours and were clearly distressed at the treatment they were receiving. These and other studies on obedience to authority, although they found many different factors to be important in predicting obedience, all led to substantially the same conclusion: ordinary people often obey orders which over-rule personal scruples and induce them to perform acts which they would otherwise find unacceptable. Whereas at one time the question posed might have been "What sort of people go on to mistreat others?", as a result of studies on conformity and obedience it has become "Under what circumstances do ordinary people go on to behave in ways which are inhumane – in ways which they would not have believed themselves capable of?"

Learning, evolution, phobias and sauce béarnaise

In Chapter 2 we talked about the experiments carried out by the Russian physiologist Pavlov (1927) in which a learned response (such as anticipatory salivation) depended on one stimulus (such as footsteps) being followed reliably by another stimulus (such as food in the mouth). This procedure has since become known as Pavlovian (or classical) conditioning. We also mentioned another form of learning (instrumental learning), associated with the name of the American psychologist Skinner (1938), where a response (such as pressing a lever) is followed by a reward (such as a pellet of food). Under these circumstances the response becomes more frequent.

For many years it was felt that learning of both these types was a relatively automatic and indiscriminate process and that animals (including humans) could learn associations equally well between all sorts of stimuli and responses. Evidence that this may not be so was first treated with considerable scepticism but experiments such as those by Garcia and Koelling (1966) slowly changed the way psychologists looked at learning. What Garcia and Koelling showed was that rats, for instance, find it relatively easy to associate tastes with later feelings of sickness (produced by a nausea-inducing compound) and so quickly learn to avoid those tastes. A strong desire to avoid is called an aversion – hence the label "aversion learning" for this process. Rats find it very difficult, however, to associate either visual stimuli or sounds with later sickness. Some birds (such as quail), on the other hand, find it much easier to associate visual stimuli with sickness but have difficulty learning which tastes are followed by feelings of nausea. One possible explanation for these differences is that the process of evolution has given animals learning abilities which are most appropriate to their lifestyles. That is, animals are "primed" or "prepared" by their evolutionary history to learn most readily about those things which are likely to be of most relevance to them. Rats identify their food primarily by taste and smell, and so it is the information from these senses which is most usefully associated with sickness. Quail, on the other hand, use vision to find food, and for them sickness is importantly linked with things seen.

The same phenomenon of "preparedness" to learn some things very quickly is also seen in humans and has been labelled by one psychologist (Seligman 1972) the "sauce béarnaise phenomenon". Seligman described how he had eaten an enjoyable meal including sauce béarnaise (egg-thickened sauce, flavoured with tarragon), went to the opera and then suffered the effects of a viral infection which had caused him to be violently sick during the night. He subsequently found that he had developed an aversion to the taste of sauce béarnaise, but not to the sight of the white plate he had eaten off in the restaurant, nor to the sound of the opera – all of which had also preceded his nocturnal nausea. It is interesting that this aversion to sauce béarnaise developed despite the fact that Seligman knew perfectly well that it had been the viral infection and not the sauce which had caused his illness, suggesting that this type of learning occurs at an involuntary level. You may also be familiar with a (usually temporary) aversion to the taste of, for example, whisky following occasions when its ingestation has been followed for whatever reason by vomiting.

In Chapter 2 we also mentioned the fear of rats which Watson and Rayner (1920) had induced in little Albert (an 11-month-old child) by associating the presence of a white rat with the fear caused by a sudden loud noise. Albert's acquired fear was also manifest as anxiety when presented with a white rabbit, a fur coat or even a Father Christmas mask. Watson felt that his experiment with the hapless Albert might provide an explanation for irrational, but nonetheless debilitating, adult fears or phobias. It is also said that Watson speculated mischievously on the possibility that if these learned anxieties were not removed Albert might as an adult, having forgotten the experiment, consult a psychoanalyst on account of his unnatural fears and be treated to the interpretation of an unresolved Oedipal conflict. This story may be apocryphal but highlights the rivalry which has sometimes existed between behaviourists like Watson and those with a more psychoanalytic view of mental problems.

If, as Watson argued, phobias are the result of associating an environmental stimulus with a fearful or painful response, we might expect a much wider range of phobias than are actually seen. The objects of most human phobias are not arbitrary. They are, according to evolutionary psychologists like Seligman, highly specific to objects or situations that might have been critical to our evolution and survival in the past. Seligman suggests we should contrast the objects of common phobias, such as the dark, heights, enclosed spaces, snakes and spiders, which may have been associated with danger in our distant evolutionary past, with more recent and household objects such as hammers, electric sockets, doors, stoves and parents. Most children suffer much more pain and injury from objects in the latter category and yet there are very few people with hammer phobias. Inbuilt evolutionary predispositions could thus be thought to be responsible for the far greater number of people with spider phobias. Indeed, there are very few of us who are not spider-phobic to some degree. Equally, a number of people in central London experience snake phobia while most have never seen a live snake. Watson had perhaps been lucky to have chosen as the basis for Albert's acquired phobia a natural object which humans have some predisposition to associate with fear and avoidance (i.e. a rat – perhaps with past associations in human history with plague and illness).

Memory and its distortions

Just as the study of learning has a long history in psychology so has its counterpart, memory. One of the major messages to emerge from all of this work is that our memories are nowhere near as accurate as we perhaps think they are. Clearly this has huge implications for the reliance we place on the validity of our own recall and, particularly in legal contexts, the testimony of eyewitnesses. Some of the early experiments were carried out by Bartlett (1932) who was interested in, among other things, how we remember stories. He used a North American folk tale "The war of the ghosts" which his English subjects read twice and were then asked to recall repeatedly over a period of several years. What Bartlett found was that even on the first recall trials some 15 minutes after reading the story, the narrative and its details began to conform to the very different cultural backgrounds, experiences and expectations of the readers. Eventually, with retelling, many of the supernatural elements of the original story were lost, the warriors in later versions fight *against* the ghosts, whereas originally the ghosts were the hero's companions, the canoes become boats and the hero dies, more dramatically perhaps, at sunset rather than at sunrise. Nevertheless one outstanding detail of the original tended to stand the test of time. One subject, two and a half years after reading the story, completed his retelling with "Something black came out of his mouth" and "He was dead". Both sentences are exactly as they appeared in the original.

We might think that just as with the dramatic detail from Bartlett's "The war of the ghosts" story, memories of dramatic events in our own lives might survive more or less unchanged. Apparently not. One study investigated people's memories of how they heard the tragic news of the 1986 explosion of the space shuttle *Challenger* (Neisser & Harsch 1992). This event clearly had a very powerful impact on those subjects selected to take part in the study, and on the morning after the explosion they gave clear and accurate accounts of what they were doing when they heard the news. Three years later, however, when they were again asked to recall how they had heard the news, none were able to give a completely accurate account and some were grossly inaccurate, although they all claimed still to have vivid memories of the event. One subject, for example, was in reality taking a business call on the telephone when a friend interrupted the call to tell her the news of the disaster. Three years later the same subject recounted confidently how she had first heard the news in a classroom and had dismissed it as a joke until she later saw the news on television.

Confidently holding false memories for something which actually happened is bad enough; worse perhaps is the holding of apparently clear memories of things which never happened. A good example of just that has been provided by the well-known developmental psychologist Piaget (1962) and concerns one of his own childhood memories. Piaget clearly recalled from his own early years the details of an attempted kidnapping in which he was involved. He had retained these memories for over 10 years when he discovered that his nanny, apparently finally overcome with guilt at having kept the watch she had received for her part in foiling the kidnapping, had confessed to making the whole thing up. Piaget's own explanation was that he must have heard the story recounted many times by his parents and others, who all believed it to be true, and that he had projected these accounts into the past and developed what were to him clear visual "memories" of the event as it was alleged to have taken place.

The nanny in Piaget's story seems to have implanted successfully, whether she intended to or not, a false memory into the child's mind which he then as an adult accepted as true and felt he could recall vividly. Recent interest in false memories has led some researchers to attempt to repeat Piaget's nanny's feat under experimental conditions. Loftus (1992) describes how she and her colleagues were able to implant false memories of being lost as a child in their subjects. The method was simple. One of the subject's family was recruited as an accomplice of the experimenter and was asked to reminisce (untruthfully) with the subject about a time when he, the subject, was lost in a shopping precinct. To take a particular example, the older brother of one of the subjects, Chris, recounted a prearranged, made-up story as follows:

It was 1981 or 1982. I remember Chris was 5. We had gone shopping at the University City shopping mall in Spokane. After some panic, we found Chris being led down the mall by a tall, oldish man (I think he was wearing a flannel shirt). Chris was crying and holding the man's hand. The man explained that he had found Chris walking around crying his eyes out just a few moments before and was trying to help him find his parents.

Over the next few days Chris was questioned about the incident, and as time went by, was able to "remember" more and more about it without any further prompting from either his family or the experimenters. Two weeks after he had first heard about the incident Chris confidently described his clear and vivid memory of it as follows:

> I was with you guys for a second and I think I went over to look at a toy store, the Kaybee toy and uh, we got lost and I was looking around and I thought "Uh-oh. I'm in trouble now." You know. And then I . . . I thought I was never going to see my family again. I was really scared you know. And then this old man, I think he was wearing a blue flannel suit, came up to me . . . he was kind of old. He was kind of bald on top . . . he had like a ring of gray hair . . . and he had glasses.

Even when Chris was eventually told that the story he had been told was untrue he seemed unwilling to deny what he now felt were real and powerful memories of it. His response to the revelation was:

> Really? I thought I remembered being lost . . . and looking round for you guys. I do remember that. And then crying. And mom coming up and saying "Where were you? Don't you . . . Don't you ever do that again."

People not only seem readily to form false memories but to believe them and then to go on to recount them vividly and confidently. In this way we can become what one researcher has called "honest liars".

Split-brains and why our passport photographs look so awful

One of the basic issues in psychology reviewed in Chapter 2 was that of mind versus body. The experimental work in this section looks at some evidence relevant to that issue. Specifically, it considers the relationship between the more advanced parts of our brains and our experience of consciousness and free will. A major feature of the human brain is that it is constructed of two symmetrical halves, particularly the higher parts – the cerebral hemispheres. The surfaces of the hemispheres are intensely wrinkled and contain the nerve cells which form the so-called "grey matter" of our brains. The appearance of the two hemispheres is similar to the two halves of a walnut. In order to understand the research considered in this section it is important to know two further things about the cerebral hemispheres. The first is that they are specialized in various ways and the second is that the two hemispheres are connected by a very large bundle of nerves known as the corpus callosum which forms a two-way information channel between them. One form of specialization is that by and large each hemisphere is responsible for functions in the opposite side of the body. So, if we look straight ahead, those things on the left side of our field of view are "seen" by the right hemisphere and those on the right are seen by the left hemisphere. Similarly, the sense of touch and the ability to move on the right side of our body as well as the sounds arriving at our right ear are dealt with in the first instance by our left hemisphere and vice versa for our right hemisphere. An additional specialization is that for most of us our ability to speak and use language is housed in our left hemisphere. Our right hemisphere by contrast is commonly better equipped to deal with spatial problems, such as sorting blocks into patterns or recognizing faces. In a very simple sense, then, what we have in our skulls is essentially a left brain and a right brain with one of these brains having a virtual monopoly on the expression of language, usually the left brain. Normally, of course, all of the information from left and right brains is linked together by the thick nerve fibres of the corpus callosum joining the two hemispheres. But what would happen if the corpus callosum was not there or was removed? Is mind an indivisible supernatural entity or would dividing our brains divide our minds? Would the left sides of our bodies be in conflict with the right? Would we only be able to speak about what was in our left hemisphere? When it came to making decisions would we be literally in two minds?

Animal studies and surgical reports of patients in which the corpus callosum was severed to provide access to tumours and abscesses in the middle of the brain generally showed very little effect on normal behaviour from cutting the corpus callosum. Additionally, in a small number of individuals the corpus callosum fails to develop properly and where this occurs in the absence of other anatomical abnormalities, intellectual capacity and general behaviour lie within the normal range. These observations led to the suggestion that cutting the corpus callosum might be used in cases of chronic epilepsy to prevent the spread of seizures from one hemisphere into the other hemisphere. Eventually this was tried and proved remarkably successful, not only in preventing the spread of epilepsy, but also in reducing its frequency even in the hemisphere which contained the focus. The procedure of cutting the corpus callosum was then adopted in some further cases of very severe epilepsy and provided a small number of so-called "split-brain" patients who were tested psychologically, especially in the late 1960s and the 1970s by Sperry, Gazzaniga and their colleagues (Gazzaniga et al. 1977; Sperry 1968 – for a review see Springer & Deutsch 1989).

Using visual stimuli presented very briefly to either the left or the right side of the visual field revealed independence of mental processing in the two hemispheres in these split-brain patients. In a very simple early test, flashes of light were presented to the left or right visual field and the patient was asked to say out loud when he saw one. The patient typically reported only those on the right, that is those detected by his linguistically able left hemisphere. If, however, he was asked to point to the lights as they occurred, he could do so accurately (using the hand on the same side as the flash) to both left- and right-sided flashes. He still reported only those on the right and said he was "guessing" when he pointed with his left hand. What seems to be happening here is that in the split-brain person the left hemisphere (or left brain) can see, can use the right hand to point to, and can tell the experimenter about, flashes of light occurring to the right of the visual field. The left brain, however, appears to be ignorant of any information arriving at the right brain. Similarly, the right hemisphere (or right brain) can detect and point (using the left hand) to light stimuli arriving from the left half of the visual field but, lacking verbal skills, cannot tell the experimenter about them.

Similarly, if a picture of an object is presented rapidly to the left brain the split-brain patient can name it immediately. If, however, an object is shown to the right brain, only a wild guess is produced (by the left brain which does its best to comply with the experimenter's request). But, under these same conditions, the left hand can search through a bag of unseen objects and select the right one and even indicate its use by means of a hand mime (e.g. stirring with a spoon). At no point throughout the whole performance, however, can the patient say what the object is. In fact, if different objects are shown, one to the left brain and one to the right brain, both hands will search through the same grab-bag of objects and each will select out its own object, discarding the object which the other hand is looking for if it happens to come across it.

This independence of the two hands has been used in less formal settings to identify split-brain individuals in the form of "the strange hand test" (Brion & Jedynak 1972). If the split-brain patient is asked to put both his hands behind his back and an experimenter surreptitiously grips the patient's right hand in his own hand, the patient recognizes that he is holding a hand but cannot tell whether it is his own or someone else's.

Though it normally cannot use speech, the right brain can understand language and shows a degree of conceptual ability. In one study involving a split-brain subject, a picture of a cigarette was presented to the right brain and the left hand sorted through a grab-bag which did not in fact contain a cigarette. The left hand instead came up with a conceptually related object – an ashtray. In a similar vein a verbal cue was presented, "Monkeys eat them", and the patient sorted through a bag of plastic fruit with his left hand until he retrieved a banana. It could be shown that the left, speaking brain was not solving the problem in this case. When the items of fruit were placed in the left hand some minutes later the patient (that is the patient's left brain) could not say what they were.

In the early post-operative stages many split-brain patients described apparent conflicts of will between the two hemispheres, until they had learned strategies to cope with them. In all of these cases when the actions were carried out by the left hand under the control of the right brain the patient (i.e. the speaking left brain) regarded them as unwilled or alien acts. One patient found that on picking up a newspaper with his right hand the left hand would put it down again. Similarly, another patient reported that on turning to the correct page in a book the left hand would turn over more pages – he took to reading whilst sitting on his left hand.

A further example of this type of conflict in a split-brain patient was caught on film during a formal testing situation. In this instance the right hand (left brain) was having difficulty with a block-sorting task, something which the left hand under the guidance of the right brain is much better at. The irritation experienced by the right brain at the inefficiency of the left brain–right-hand team could be witnessed in the left hand's agitated movements. Eventually the left hand was seen reaching across and solving the problem. The patient in this situation was surprised by the action of the left hand – but grateful for the help. If the experimenters wanted to test the right hand on its own they had to hold down the patient's left hand.

A further example (given by Dimond 1979) is worth quoting in a split-brain patient's own words as she describes some of the things her left hand has done. Remember "the patient" is represented by her speaking left brain and its associated right hand. We do not know what the patient's right brain thinks about all of this, as it is unable to express itself in speech, though we can infer some things from the actions of the left hand.

> You wouldn't want to hear some of the things this left hand has done – you wouldn't believe it. It acts independently a lot of times. I don't even tell it to – I don't know it is going to do anything. Sometimes I go to get something with my right hand, the left hand grabs it and stops it – for some reason. Things – this hand is uncontrollable. It seems to have a mind of its own. Sometimes, to my dismay, it gets up and slaps me. Sometimes in the morning I wake up at a certain hour – I don't have a clock in the bedroom – I have a clock in the kitchen – and that left hand slaps me awake – boy, sometimes it gets out of hand. Look what happened – what happened was somebody slapped me. It was my left hand all the time. I was asleep, completely asleep, then all of

a sudden – slap – the left hand slapped me awake. In other words I usually wake up at a certain hour just automatically – I guess I've had my rest for the night. When I've had enough sleep I wake up – but this one morning – one morning the left hand for some reason – it was 15 minutes after 6 and I usually wake up right at 6 – Whang! That left hand slapped me awake – I'm getting violent with myself. My Gosh!

This quotation also illustrates some other things which have been reported about split-brain patients.
- They have a curious sense of humour. Puns and quips are characteristic of the linguistically more able left brain. (The right brain is often considered to be the more depressive of the two.)
- Sleep may not be simultaneous in the two brains. (The right brain is the one which may control dreams.)
- The left hand and the right brain are considered "not me". "She", the patient with a will of her own, is the left brain.
- Two independent and apparently rich sets of consciousnesses (personalities even) are co-existing in the two brains.

These results are obviously of some significance for our understanding of consciousness and of the relationship between brain and mind. They suggest that consciousness, free will, thought and cognitive processes generally are firmly bedded in the physical structure of the brain and do not transcend physical boundaries. The two "brains" in the skull of a split-brain patient seem to be in no greater communication than your brain is with that of a person standing next to you.

As a tailpiece to this consideration of some aspects of neuropsychology it is worth looking at a more everyday example of the effects of specialization between our two cerebral hemispheres. One ability which our right hemispheres seem to excel in is that of recognizing faces. This means that recognition of others is based mainly on the right side of their face, which fills the left side of our visual field (and hence reaches our right hemisphere) when we face them. In fact this can be shown to be the case by taking a full-face photograph of someone we know and making a second print of it but reversed left to right, so that it is a mirror image. If we now cut both the original and the reversed photograph vertically into left and right halves we can then recombine the images as two "right" sides and two "left" sides. The reconstituted face consisting of two right halves is much more recognizable as the original person than the one consisting of two left sides. The latter, by contrast, is often seen as more "emotional" and it has been suggested that emotions are expressed more by the left sides of our faces than the right (Sackheim et al. 1978).

So much for other people's faces and their photographs but what about the way we recognize our own face? On a daily basis our experience of our own appearance is gleaned from mirror gazing. In a mirror, however, it is the *left* side of our face which falls into the left half of our visual field and is presumably recognized by the right hemisphere. On the other hand, when we look at a photograph of ourselves, it is the right side of our face which the face-recognition system in our right hemisphere encounters. This may explain why we feel that photographs, particularly the full-face photographs needed for passports, do not really look like us – or at least not the "us" we are familiar with on looking in the mirror in the morning. Other people, however, who are used to recognizing the right sides of our faces, are apt to tell us that the photograph is a good likeness. As a result of our particular cerebral specialization, therefore, the person we recognize as ourself in a mirror may not be the person others see.

Unconscious signals: noses and eyes

Speech is one of the more obvious ways in which we communicate with our fellow human beings. Some forms of communication take place without words, however, and sometimes without our being consciously aware of them. These may be the older forms of communication from our pre-verbal past and which we share with other animals. Among the most potent of signals are the chemicals detected by taste and odour and collectively known as pheromones. Pheromones are used within a species to signal sex, status, group membership, etc., as well as marking trails and defining territories. A familiar example of the latter is dogs urinating on strategically placed objects such as lamp posts and, in the case of one in our own neighbourhood, garage door handles.

In humans the power of pheromones is presumably reflected by the perfume industry which uses extracts from the odour glands of a variety of species, or their synthetic equivalents, as a basis for its products. One of these is musk – a reddish brown substance secreted by glands located in a very appropriate part of the anatomy of the male musk deer. It seems likely that we share the sexual signal value of musk as most human females detect musk substances which men do not, although human males are able to detect musk-like odours if they are injected with the female hormone oestrogen. The woman's sensitivity to musk also varies with the menstrual cycle.

Consistent with the view that human males may transmit a musk-like pheromone which they cannot detect themselves is the charming story related by Eibl-Eibesfeldt (1971) who noted that in some (unspecified) Mediterranean countries it is the traditional practice of young men at dances to wave a small kerchief in front of the face of the girl of their choice. Before the dance the kerchiefs are worn close to the body – particularly under the armpit. – presumably to impregnate it with the male pheromone. In modern society, females are sensitive to, and frequently object to, male body odour – possibly as a result of a cultural trend towards cleanliness, but also the wearing of clothes may allow bacteriological action to convert the pheromone to a less pleasant compound. Above all, it is important to recognize that the human underarm is a glandular area giving out substances of a very particular odour. It was presumably not evolved to sustain the deodorant industry. The recent development of the perfume industry in giving musk-based perfumes back to men may be doing no more than returning the situation to an evolutionary status quo.

In addition to sexual messages, many mammals seem to recognize their own siblings, parents and offspring by smell. In a similar way, a study by Porter & Moore (1981) on humans has shown that not only mothers but also fathers and siblings can recognize individual children within the family by smell. The children wore the same T-shirt for three nights. The other members of the family were then invited to sniff at it through a small hole in the top of a sealed plastic container and to identify the child who had worn it. This they were able to do. Some of the difference in human skin odour depends on diet but the fact that children within the same family can be distinguished by their parents by smell alone suggests an individual, genetically based mechanism.

The eyes also provide a powerful medium for transmitting both consciously and unconsciously generated messages. One way in which this can be done is by variation in the size of our pupils – the black apertures in the centre of our eyes. In order to control the amount of light entering the eye the pupils of our eyes increase in size (dilate) in the dark and constrict in the light. Other circumstances affect pupil size, however. For instance, when we are aroused or interested, our pupils dilate – a fact which has been used by poker players, Chinese jade dealers, Turkish rug sellers and, no doubt, double-glazing salesmen to their own advantage. The sudden, involuntary enlarging of our pupils when we are dealt an unbeatable hand of cards may defeat the impression of nonchalance which our "poker face" is intended to convey. The incidence of eye shades and dark glasses in these circumstances is a useful counter-ploy to keep the pupils dilated throughout.

The signals from pupil-size changes might be used consciously or unconsciously by the various players in the different situations suggested above. When it comes to signalling attractiveness, however, there is experimental evidence to suggest that the signalling power of pupil size works unconsciously.

Hess (1975) found that men rated as more attractive a photograph of a girl in which the pupils had been artificially enlarged than they did the identical photo but with the pupils diminished in size. The subjects did not report seeing the difference in pupil size. This suggests a signal operating unconsciously to indicate mutual interest. The pupil-size effect may explain why candlelit meals are considered so romantic (the low-light conditions ensure that our pupils are attractively dilated). In a similar way, the drug belladonna has been used over the centuries by women wishing to attract men, or their money. Belladonna (literally, "beautiful lady") is an extract of deadly nightshade, containing atropine, which mimics the arousing effect of the sympathetic nervous system, and dilates the pupil when instilled into the eye.

A less commonly acknowledged facial signal, but one which has been found by psychologists across a variety of human cultures is the eyebrow flash (Eibl-Eibesfeldt 1971). The eyebrows are jerked upwards for about one-sixth of a second – accompanied often by a nod of the head, a widening of the eyes and a smile. This serves universally as a friendly (sometimes flirtatious) greeting at a distance. You may not be aware of the number of times you use the eyebrow flash yourself. Take a mental note next time you are out in company or when you pass an acquaintance in the street – you may be surprised. You might also like to ponder the question "Which came first, the eyebrow or the flash?" Or, to put it another way, "Why did human eyebrows evolve?" A traditional explanation is that they serve to deflect sweat from the eyes. The discovery of the eyebrow-flash signal suggests another explanation – that they are there to accentuate part of our non-verbal signalling system. Rather like the unusually enlarged claw which the fiddler crab waves aloft as a signal to others across a crowded shore.

Freud, the unconscious and awareness under anaesthesia

We noted in Chapter 2 that one of Freud's contributions to psychological thought was the view that much of our behaviour stems from processes which are unconscious (i.e. that the person is unaware of). Inborn instincts, particularly those relating to sex and aggression, give rise to impulses which are forbidden or are punished by parents and/or society at large.

These repressive elements force the impulses out of awareness and into the unconscious where they remain and may, for example, influence the content of dreams, cause slips of the tongue (Freudian slips) or memory lapses (Freudian errors). The latter two phenomena are "errors" which have a genuine, but unconscious, motive or meaning. Leaving behind one's hat or gloves at a particular person's house, for instance, may betray an unconscious wish to meet that person again (even though at a conscious level one may be indifferent to or even dislike the person). One of Freud's (1901) own examples concerns a young woman complaining about the disadvantages of being a woman, who said: "A woman must be pretty if she is to please the men. A man is much better off. As long as he has *five straight limbs* he needs no more."

Freud explained that this error arose from the fusion of two elements of the then familiar phrase *four straight limbs and five senses*. Importantly, however, he went on to say that the "error" would not have occurred if it did not express an unconscious idea which the young woman would consciously have preferred to have concealed. Freud offers the young woman's embarrassment at realizing what she has said as evidence that this was an honest (albeit unconsciously motivated) slip of the tongue and not simply either a verbal confusion or an attempt at a slightly smutty joke.

Repressed, unconscious impulses may also create emotional problems and symptoms of mental illness, or may emerge in socially acceptable ways in art or literature. In his book on Leonardo da Vinci, for example, Freud (1910) suggested that da Vinci's fascination with painting madonnas was a veiled expression of his desire for his mother, which had been frustrated at an early age as a result of being separated from her.

One of the criticisms levelled at Freudian theory is that it is very difficult to test, particularly when unconscious material (which by definition even the subject is not able to access) is claimed to be influencing behaviour or attitudes. A person may say (and believe) that he loves his father but it is always open to the Freudian analyst to say (without any possibility of being proved right or wrong) that really, unconsciously, that person is jealous of the father's relationship with the mother and that this is the reason for the anxiety or guilty feelings. There are other situations, however, where it has been possible to demonstrate a relationship between unconscious mental processes and behaviour. The particular examples to be given here involve information processing while the individual is anaesthetized.

Surgical-depth anaesthesia produces lack of response during painful procedures and patients show no memory of the period during which they were anaesthetized. There is evidence, however, that anaesthetized patients hear and understand much of what goes on (particularly when it relates specifically to them), and that this material is stored unconsciously and can affect both attitudes and recovery from surgery. Cheek & Le Cron (1968), for example, in a review of earlier studies reported a female patient who refused to go back to her surgeon for reasons she could not understand. She had liked him before the operation. Under hypnosis the woman was later able to quote the surgeon as saying while she was anaesthetized "Well, that will take care of this old bag!" In another case a woman undergoing plastic surgery on her face, after an automobile accident, was found to have a lump on her lip. The surgeon commented "My gracious" (or words to that effect) "this is not a cyst. It could be cancer." The woman recalled nothing of the operation but became more and more depressed after her surgery, lost weight and could no longer sleep. Three months after the operation she was hypnotized and was able to recall the remark made by the surgeon at the time but changed the word "cancer" to "malignant". This revelation, plus the information that a subsequent lab test had shown the lump to be non-cancerous, was followed by a marked improvement in the woman's physical and mental condition.

Cheek & Le Cron's review included a study by Levinson (1965) in which the question of information processing under anaesthesia had been subjected to more formal testing using a procedure involving a faked "emergency" in the operating room. Ten patients who were undergoing routine surgery were selected but were told nothing of the purpose of the study. When EEG and other measures indicated that a surgical plane of anaesthesia had been achieved, the anaesthetist by prior arrangement told the surgeon to wait, as the patient looked as if he needed more oxygen, his lips were blue, etc. A period of apparently urgent activity followed, centred on the anaesthetic machine, and the anaesthetist then closed the experimental episode by announcing that the patient now looked all right. Despite the customary claims of complete post-operative amnesia, under hypnosis four of the patients were later able to repeat the conversation exactly as it had occurred and showed alarm as they relived the experience. Four others awoke from the hypnosis in anxiety at the point at which the incident occurred. "He's saying my colour is grey . . . He's going to give me some oxygen . . . He said I will be all right now . . . They're going to start again now. I can feel him bending close to me."

These experiments seem to show not only that patients are able to process information at an unconscious level during surgical anaesthesia but that this information can, if it is negative in nature, adversely affect their recovery. This is true even though the patients cannot recall the information when the anaesthetic has worn off. Fortunately the same process can lead to more positive outcomes. For example, Bonke and his colleagues (1986) showed that exposure to positive suggestions during general anaesthesia, as compared to noise or operating theatre sounds, enabled patients to recover more quickly and to avoid the necessity for a prolonged post-operative stay in hospital.

Multiple personality, hypnosis and the hidden observer

For this set of examples we stay with the question of divisions between what is conscious and what is unconscious but we also look at divisions *within* consciousness. In the earlier discussion of split-brains we saw how consciousness could apparently be divided physically by a surgeon's knife; and in the previous section, that areas of experience could be separated by anaesthesia. In this section the examples involve divisions of consciousness in normal, intact brains. That is, the divisions in awareness are psychological, or "functional", rather than being caused by some physical means.

It is quite common for whole sequences of highly complex and skilled activities, which in the early stages of their development required our close attention and filled the mainstream of our consciousness, to become automatic and separated from awareness later. Driving a car is the classic example where not only the mechanisms of driving and gear changing, but also negotiating traffic and route finding, can be so automated that the driver can carry on a conversation without awareness of driving – indeed may travel long distances with no recollection afterwards of large parts of the journey, of landmarks passed, etc. If an unusual situation arises, however, the conversation is interrupted and driving becomes the focus of attention.

One way of describing phenomena of this sort is to suggest that these automated mental activities have become dissociated – a term coined by Pierre Janet (1889). Even more extreme forms of dissociation may involve the whole personality leading to the clinical condition known as multiple-personality disorder.

Probably the best-known popular example of multiple-personality disorder from recent television and cinema representations of the story is that of Sybil (Schreiber 1973). Sybil had 16 separate personalities, including 2 males who did the carpentry and other odd jobs while Sybil was "away". A particularly important insight which arises from the Sybil story as it unfolds is that each of the personalities emerged during her development to solve some crisis in her life. Childhood abuse figures frequently in the case histories of multiple personalities. It is as though a separate set of awarenesses with their associated memories are dissociated in the form of a secondary personality to deal with and keep separate the painful experiences. Once this has happened the process may be repeated when other problems threaten the child.

One of the best-documented cases of multiple-personality disorder from the clinical research literature is that of Jonah (Brandsma & Ludwig 1974) who had four personalities:

- *Jonah*. A black 27-year old. The primary personality, shy, retiring, polite and conventional (The Square). Frightened and confused during interviews. Jonah is unaware of the other three personalities. He has been in trouble with the police for violent behaviour which he denies all knowledge of.
- *Sammy*. Sammy has the most intact memories and is aware of all four personalities. Sammy emerges when Jonah needs legal advice or is in trouble (The Mediator). Sammy remembers emerging at the age of 6 when Jonah's mother stabbed his stepfather and Sammy persuaded his parents never to fight again in front of the children.
- *King Young*. Emerged when Jonah was 6 or 7 to straighten out his sexual identity when Jonah's mother dressed him up from time to time in girls' clothing at home. King Young (The Lover) emerges

whenever Jonah needs assistance in achieving sexual gratification with women. King Young is aware of the other personalities but only dimly. Sadly Jonah, as we said, is not aware of King Young's experiences.

- *Usoffa Abdulla*. A cold, belligerent angry person who is sworn to protect Jonah (he is The Warrior). He emerged at age 9–10 when some white boys beat up Jonah who was helpless. When Usoffa emerged, however, he fought viciously against the attackers. He is also dimly aware of the other personalities.

One feature of multiple personalities is that they are usually good hypnotic subjects and the different personalities can be called out under hypnosis. Some have gone so far as to suggest that multiple personality is a product of self-hypnosis (Bliss 1986). The clinicians investigating Jonah learned from Sammy under hypnosis that a new personality was forming and was far more terrible than Usoffa (to their relief he never emerged during their sessions). They labelled this nascent personality De Nova. Self-portraits drawn by each of the four personalities differed in style and reflected their appointed roles. Personality and other tests revealed significant differences on items which were emotionally loaded but all personalities scored similarly on intelligence and vocabulary tests.

The suggestion that multiple-personality disorder may be related to processes akin to self-hypnosis may receive some support from the fact that similar dissociative phenomena can be induced in normal subjects using hypnosis. One such phenomenon, the "hidden observer" was discovered by accident (Hilgard 1977) during a classroom demonstration of hypnotic deafness. The hypnotized subject was told that on a count of three he would be deaf and would not hear again until the hypnotist placed a hand on the subject's shoulder. The subject gave every appearance of being profoundly deaf, ignoring loud noises, insults, etc. At this point a member of the audience asked "Is it possible that some part of the subject's mind still knows what is going on?" The hypnotist then asked the still deaf subject to raise a finger if this was true. To most people's surprise a finger rose in acknowledgement. While this was going on the subject had heard nothing since the word "three". In fact, as he later told the experimenter, he was making the most of the peaceful interlude and was calmly puzzling over a statistics problem when he noticed his finger rising and he wanted to know why.

The hypnotist did not explain immediately but restored the subject's hearing and suggested that when his, the hypnotist's, hand was placed on the subject's arm the same part of his mind that knew about the finger raising would be able to speak. On placing the hand, the subject was able to recall all that had gone on during his deafness including the question from the audience and the reason for the finger raising. With the hand removed again, however, the hypnotized subject once more had no memory of either what had happened during his deafness or of what he had said when the hypnotist's hand was on his arm. By this stage the subject was urgently demanding answers. A suggestion for full recall of all that had happened was given and this enabled the subject to retrieve both sets of information.

In this situation there seems to be an area of consciousness, since labelled the "hidden observer", which is monitoring the whole experience, is in a sense not hypnotized, and can be made to alternate in awareness with the hypnotized part of the subject. Hidden-observer-like phenomena had in fact been described previously but usually in the guise of "automatic writing" or "automatic signalling". Kaplan (1960), for example, hypnotized a subject and used suggestions to make the subjects' left hand insensitive. Prior to the hypnosis, automatic-writing instructions had been given – the subject had been told that his right hand would be free to write without conscious awareness of what it was communicating. Kaplan then pricked the subject's left hand three times with a hypodermic needle – the left hand showed no reaction. However, the right hand began to write hurriedly – "Ouch, damn it, you're hurting me." A few moments later the subject asked Kaplan "in all innocence" when the experiment was going to begin. In this situation again the hidden observer was monitoring all that was happening – including the pain of the needle pricks – and was able to report it (via the right hand) without the subject himself being aware of what was being communicated.

In a similar way, surgery can be carried out under hypnotic analgesia (loss of awareness of pain sensation) and an account of the pain can be retrieved later by adopting a hidden-observer strategy. Chertok (1981), for instance, reports on a Mrs D who underwent an operation to remove a small cyst in her left wrist and a foreign body in her right index finger. Mrs D displayed good hypnotic analgesia and showed post-hypnotic amnesia. That is, she appeared oblivious of the operation and of the operating room and did not recall anything about the procedure afterwards. When hypnotized again, Mrs D was able to recall the people in the operating room, the numbness of her arms and the fact that she had asked for, and received, a drink of water. During surgery she had been thinking mainly of a holiday and had re-experienced the sun shining as she sailed in a pedal-craft. At this stage, however, she reported feeling nothing of the operation. Upon a suggestion designed to call upon the hidden observer, however, she stated: "The thermocautery was so hot . . . It was burning . . . it was agony . . . as bad as the incision".

The hidden observer had clearly monitored the situation and had kept to itself (or herself) the painful experiences – somewhat like the role of a secondary personality in the multiple-personality cases.

Autism and the theory of mind

Autism is a relatively rare but often quite severe mental disorder, occurring in about 4 children in every 10,000 (Happé 1994). A major problem which autistic children have is in coping with social situations, though some of them are of normal intelligence. They also have particular difficulties in "pretend play" and tend to treat people and objects alike. For many years this pattern of problems could not be explained very convincingly. More recently, however, it has been suggested that the autistic child's difficulty is that it either cannot, or does not, understand that people have independent minds and that they know, want, feel or believe different things. In particular, the autistic child may not understand that the contents of its own mind can be different from those of other people. They do not, in other words, have a "theory of mind" (Baron-Cohen et al. 1985). One way of testing this possibility has been to engage various types of children in a play scene enacted with dolls and then to ask questions which can only be answered correctly if the child appreciates not only that other people have minds but that the contents of other people's minds can differ from their own. The children tested were autistic children of relatively normal intelligence, Down's syndrome children who were the same age but of lower intelligence, and a group of younger normal children. There were two dolls, Sally and Anne, a marble, a basket and a brown plastic box. The experimenter moved the dolls and the marble appropriately as the story unfolded in front of the child. The story went as follows:

> This is Sally and this is Anne. Anne has a basket and Sally has a brown plastic box. Anne has a marble in her basket. Anne goes for a walk. Sally goes over to Anne's basket, takes her marble, and puts it into her box. Anne comes back from her walk.

The experimenter then asked the child: "Where will Anne look for her marble?"

The predicted difference between the children emerged. The Down's syndrome and the normal children all pointed to where Anne mistakenly believed the marble to be – in her basket. In contrast, most of the autistic children, despite their higher IQ, pointed to the box, where the marble really was. Thus the autistic children failed to demonstrate that another person might have a different belief about a situation – they failed to demonstrate "a theory of mind". They really do not appear to understand what other people are thinking. It is little wonder then that they have difficulty in dealing with social situations and cannot differentiate what is pretend from what is real. The hope is that research of this type will bring us closer to an understanding of what makes autistic children "tick" and what kind of treatment they most need.

Fried grasshoppers revisited

And finally, the answer to the question posed earlier: The people who ate the grasshoppers for the unpleasant experimenter later reported a greater liking for fried grasshoppers. Why? The explanation goes as follows:

The two main cognitions involved for both groups are initially unbalanced:

A. "The idea of eating fried grasshoppers is distasteful" and B. "I ate fried grasshoppers".

For the "pleasant experimenter" group there is the balancing cognition C, "I ate them because the experimenter was really nice and asked me to", which means no change is needed to cognitions A and B. This group can continue to hold the belief that eating fried grasshoppers is distasteful.

For the "unpleasant experimenter" group the corresponding cognition C, "I ate them even though I didn't like the experimenter" hardly justifies the act and so does not achieve mental balance. A further mental adjustment was needed and so cognition A changed to produce the balanced set:

A. "The idea of eating fried grasshoppers is really quite attractive". B." I ate fried grasshoppers" C. "I ate them even though I didn't like the experimenter".

Following on

You will find references to the original sources of all the examples given in this chapter in the reference list at the end of the book. If you find any of the studies we have mentioned particularly interesting you might like to look at the original reports, although some of them may take a lot of finding. At this stage it would probably be more useful for you to look at one of the general textbooks in psychology which we list in Chapter 6. You will discover that there are many more experiments to consider in the areas which we have mentioned. Most of the famous studies reported here have been replicated and followed up by researchers more recently. The textbooks we have suggested will give you other references which may be more easy to get hold of. They will also give you an idea of the many areas which we haven't covered here. Remember, it is not our suggestion that you read a textbook from cover to cover. Rather that you browse through it, reading those sections which look as though they might interest you particularly. That way you will begin to gain an insight into the sheer breadth of our subject.

Chapter 5
Uses (and possible abuses)
of psychology

Introduction

The aim of psychology is to *describe, understand* and *explain* behaviour. A full understanding of the mind would allow for accurate *prediction* of behaviour. It would also allow for the *control* of human behaviour – the manipulation of the mind. Of course, being able to control behaviour means that psychological knowledge could be used for good as well as evil. Being able to detect people not telling the truth by means of a *lie detector* or some other device would be useful to the police or lawyers in their attempts to detect criminals but it may also be used by criminals to gain vital information from people whom they had kidnapped.

Therefore, there are just as many possible advantages and applications of new knowledge as disadvantages. Consider, for example, our understanding of interpersonal behaviour. From what psychologists know about verbal and non-verbal communication, they can teach people to be better communicators by using social skills, self-presentational and assertiveness training. This may help people in their private and professional lives. These social skills may considerably help people train to become better interviewers, salesmen, therapists, counsellors, teachers, public speakers, supervisors and managers. But giving people new knowledge of interpersonal behaviour may have various undesirable consequences. First, their behaviour may become more artificial and insincere – more like acting than being oneself. Secondly, they may become self-conscious, awkward and unspontaneous during the learning of the skills. Thirdly, people may be manipulated by practitioners of the new skills – for instance, they may be persuaded to buy things they neither want nor can afford; or they may put undue trust in teachers or therapists.

Knowledge is power, and its application may be used wisely or unwisely. This chapter is about the application of psychological theories and knowledge to advertising, education, industry, medicine, politics, etc., and looks at how effective various attempts to change behaviour are. Today there are *educational* psychologists, *industrial* psychologists, *clinical* psychologists, *consumer* psychologists, *engineering* psychologists, *environmental* psychologists, *medical* psychologists, *forensic* psychologists, *sports* psychologists, *military* psychologists, etc., all of whom are trained to specialize in certain areas of human behaviour. The application of psychological theories influences us considerably in our daily lives.

Psychology of sales: consumer behaviour

We are all bombarded with hundreds of advertisements every day – on the radio and television; in newspapers and magazines; on billboards and in shops. What determines whether we even attend to them, let alone follow their advice?

Consumer psychologists are interested partly in the effectiveness of the communication link between the producers and consumers of goods. Through large surveys, as well as in-depth marketing interviews and tests, psychologists hope to uncover attitudes and feelings towards products as well as unconscious motives for purchasing or not purchasing. They also note, through the behavioural approach, what people actually do. Numerous methods include analysis of sales records; actual observations of purchases (who, when, where purchases are made); people's ability to identify and distinguish between various brands; and analysis of coupon returns, etc.

In order to understand the purchasing process one needs to know about three things: the *consumer* – their personality, socio-economic class, age, sex, ethnic-group membership, buying habits and brand loyalty (each of these variables affects why, where, with whom, with how much they shop for goods); the *product* – its package (which may reflect convenience, security, status, dependability or beauty), its image and its price; and the *advertising message* – the medium it is delivered in, which needs it is appealing to, whether it is positive (pleasant consequences of purchasing the product) or negative (unpleasant consequences of not purchasing the product).

The voluminous research in this area matches the amount of money that can be made in the world of business (Wilkie 1990). But to mention just three interesting and relevant areas: the nature of persuasive messages; the most effective medium for advertising; and the possible effects of subliminal perception.

Persuasive advertising messages are written, spoken, televised and filmed to present us with facts and arguments to attempt to alter (or sometimes maintain) our attitudes to buying. Perhaps the most important aspect of the message is credibility, trustworthiness or believability. A consumer's perception of credibility is based upon the advertiser's or communicator's apparent expertise (knowledge, experience) *and* their motives (what they lose or gain). Communicators (people who endorse products) who are *high* in expertise *and* have *positive* motives are seen to be credible and are, as a result, quite successful at persuasion while the reverse is true as well – people with little expertise and questionable (selfish) motives have low credibility and are not persuasive. Thus, if top sportsmen recommend a sporting product they use, and because they are so rich appear not to do so for the money but because they believe in the product, people are more likely to buy.

Of course, the clarity, forcefulness or memorableness of the advertisement are also important. It seems that adverts that present a balanced, argued view which attempts to demolish the opposition are more effective in changing attitudes than simple one-sided arguments. What about stimulating strong emotions like anger, anxiety or fear among viewers or readers? It appears that such fear-inducing adverts (e.g. against germs) are most successful in altering attitudes if: (a) they generate *moderate* levels of emotional arousal (if too weak, they have little impact; if too strong, they are often ignored); (b) the persons who see/watch/hear them believe that the dangers cited are *real*; and (c) if they also believe that the recommendations for avoiding these dangers (i.e. using the product) will be effective.

Is it better to advertise on the television, on the radio, in newspapers and magazines, or on billboards? Factors such as cost and audience determine this decision just as much as effectiveness. Television not only costs more than radio (to produce and broadcast) but it reaches a different audience. The sex, age, socio-economic status, etc. of audiences vary enormously and wise advertisers choose their medium carefully. But there have been a number of psychological studies looking at such things as one's memory for the same material presented in newspapers and magazines (print), radio (audio) and television (audio-visual). Many people believe that an audience tends to remember *most* information received through the television and *least* through the print medium. There is accumulating evidence from various research studies, however, that this is not the case (Gunter 1987). Learning from television news is inferior to learning from newsprint. There are a variety of explanations as to why this is so. Partly it has to do with the way each medium is used by the public, but partly also it is linked with inherent characteristics of audio-visual and written materials and the way they are cognitively processed by individuals.

The fact that more learning seems to occur from newspapers than from the broadcast media of radio or television may indicate something about the inherent capacities of these different media to convey knowledge to their respective consumers. One study, for example, reported that 57 per cent of a survey sample were able to recall, in fairly complete detail, news stories they had read about in the newspapers during the previous 24 hours, whereas only about 45 per cent could recall stories seen on television equally well. How can different levels of information recall from these two media be explained?

One explanation may lie with the way news is presented in newspapers compared with on the broadcast media. Newspapers can cover stories in much more detail than radio or television news bulletins are able to. News broadcasts have restricted airtime. The narrative of a standard 25–30 minute television bulletin, for instance, carries less content than the front page of a serious broadsheet newspaper.

Another reason for different recall from print and broadcast media may be that newspaper reading is self-paced whereas on radio and television the rate at which the news is presented is determined by the programme-maker. The listener or viewer has no opportunity, once an item has been presented, to go back over it again and check details. Despite this, experimental studies in which the same materials have been presented audio-visually, in audio only or in print, and where exposure time is equated across viewers, listeners or readers, have found different levels of recall of the same stories from different modalities. Of course, remembering an advertisement is different from buying a product. But the research does seem to show that if you want to teach people something the best medium remains the printed page.

Does information through hidden messages and *subliminal* advertising work? The idea of subliminal perception is that stimuli (pictures, sounds, etc.) which are too weak or too briefly presented to enter conscious experience may, nevertheless, affect people's nervous system and thereby influence various aspects of their behaviour. That is, although people may not be aware of the stimuli (e.g. a split-second picture of a nude) their responses are qualitatively quite different from those elicited by the same stimulus when presented above the awareness threshold. Subliminal stimulation has been shown to affect dreams, memory, conscious perception, verbal behaviour and emotional responses.

In the late 1950s people became aware of the possible commercial and political gains by use of subliminal stimulation. In a now famous book published thirty years ago (*The hidden persuaders*), Vance Packard noted the possibility that advertisers were using subliminal messages to help sell their products. The idea caused outrage and stimulated considerable debate. Can a subliminal advertisement ("Eat more popcorn") or political slogan ("Vote Conservative") make someone (or at least encourage someone to) do something which he might otherwise refrain from doing? Some experimental evidence seems to suggest that this is a possibility, but there are three good reasons to suppose that it is rarely, if ever, effective. First, there are enormous individual differences in the thresholds of awareness. It is impossible to find an intensity or duration value for the "subliminal" advertisement to be subliminal at all without missing out on some people altogether. Age, and position relative to the screen, would probably alone be sufficient to account for the advert being below the physiological threshold for a sizeable proportion of the audience. A second factor is distraction and selective attention. For sublimination perception to work, the viewer needs to be in a relaxed and passive state. Because one cannot attend to a stimulus of which one is unaware, any other ongoing supra-liminal (above threshold) stimulation to which one may direct attention will almost certainly swamp any effect of a simultaneously presented sub-liminal advertisement. Thus, if a sub- and supra-liminal stimulus are presented together, the latter often swamps the former. It is very easy to prevent a weak stimulus having an effect upon behaviour.

Finally, whereas a subliminal advertisement may affect verbal behaviour (stated preferences), it is unlikely to have any major effect on other overt acts of choice. For instance, in one study subjects were shown the word "Beef" for 1/200 second, every 7 seconds, during the course of watching a supra-liminal film. Following this they rated themselves for hunger and were then encouraged to choose one from an assortment of different sandwiches. The results showed that, whereas the subliminal stimulus word "Beef" had a significant effect upon subsequent hunger-ratings, it did not affect subsequent choice behaviour. There was no significant preference for beef sandwiches. Evidently, feelings of hunger were increased, but without any discernible effect upon existing food preferences. Attractive though the technique may seem to advertisers, none of us have to be afraid of the power of these hidden persuaders.

Helping the mentally ill: clinical psychology

Mental illness may be the worst epidemic of all time. One in every ten people in the United Kingdom will at some time have to be treated for mental illness. Many others self-medicate with alcohol, drugs, tranquilizers. Some consult astrologers, their family doctor, herbalists, a local priest, while many others go to psychologists or psychiatrists. They are all seeking relief from distress – a healing of a sick mind.

It is well known that diagnosis in mental illness is difficult and unreliable because there are no sharp distinctions between normal and abnormal, and what is abnormal in one culture or situation may be normal or adaptive in another. There are, of course, various practical, everyday criteria for judging mental illness: *discomfort* in the form of physical aches, pains, nausea and fatigue as well as psychological worry, depression and anxiety; *bizarreness* in the forms of mis-perceptions of reality (hallucination by seeing, hearing, feeling what is not there); *delusions* in the misinterpretations of events and others' behaviour; *disorientation* in not knowing the date, month, year or place; and *inefficiency* in carrying out one's daily duties.

In general, there are four traditional types of mental illness: neuroses, psychoses, psychosomatic and personality disorders. *Neuroses* are commonly divided into *syndromes*, but include the following symptoms: (a) worry, tension and distractibility – indicators of excessive fear, (b) excessive forgetting, obsessive thoughts and compulsive rituals – self-defeating attempts to cope with fearful situations, (c) depression and fatigue – psychological residuals of prolonged tension. Neurotics tend to be overinhibited, anxious or guilt-ridden, and these tendencies hinder them in solving everyday problems. Neurotics tend to vacillate, be rather devious, yet be very timid. Thus neurosis is characterized by strong feelings of *anxiety*. Specific neurotic types include *anxiety neurosis* (an intense level of anxiety that interferes with all activities); *phobias* (an intense, constant and irrational fear of some object or situation); *obsessions* and *compulsions* (persistent ideas (obsessions) or behaviours (compulsions) that the person must think about or act out constantly); *hysteria*, manifested as *conversion reactions* (the conversion of some psychological disturbance into a physical disturbance such as blindness or paralysis) or *dissociative reactions* (the dissociation of parts of the personality in the form of amnesia, somnambulism or multiple personality); *hypochondria* (extreme and exaggerated concern for one's health and physical condition) and related compulsions like *kleptomania* (stealing) and *pyromania* (setting fire to things); and *depressive neurosis* (powerful, persistent and compelling feelings of depression, gloom, discouragement and rejection).

Psychoses comprise much more deviant and serious symptoms. These include: (a) hallucinations – disturbances in perceiving reality, (b) delusions – disturbances in interpreting reality, (c) free associations, fragmented and incoherent speech – disturbances of thought and expression, (d) prolonged melancholy or elation – severe and swift disturbances of mood, (e) isolation and withdrawal from others – disturbances in personal interaction patterns. Psychoses are the most severe forms of mental illness. Psychotics, who are legally labelled "insane", tend to maintain little contact with reality, live in a personal fantasy world and usually have to be hospitalized. The two major categories of psychoses are organic psychoses, caused by physical damage to the brain, and functional psychoses, caused by psychological factors such as a very disturbed childhood. Three major functional psychoses are *schizophrenia*, the splitting of the personality from reality and of the thought processes from the emotions; *manic-depressive psychosis*, extreme fluctuations of moods and feelings from the depths of depression to extreme mania and euphoria; and the *paranoid* reactions which include delusions of grandeur and persecution.

Psychosomatic disorders consist of bodily disorders usually produced by enduring states of stress: high blood pressure, skin problems, ulcers, asthma, etc. In contrast to medical illnesses, psychosomatic disorders cannot be explained solely by biological variables. It has been suggested that both heart attacks and cancer may have important psychological factors.

Personality disorders include behaviours that involve violations of the rules of society: addiction to alcohol or drugs; sex deviations; delinquency, criminality. Those who exhibit such behaviours are usually described as impetuous, weak, immoral and unrepentant; they are usually unable or unwilling to inhibit forbidden responses in the absence of a punitive person or law.

There are several approaches to helping the mentally ill. Some therapies focus on *unconscious motives*, others on *subjective feelings* and others still on *actual* behaviours. Some therapies are very "medical" in nature, such as shock therapy, drug therapy or even psychosurgery. They are aimed at management rather than cure and are often last resorts for attempting radical behaviour changes or symptom relief. There are also various types of individual psychotherapy aimed at giving patients self-insight into personal problems and providing them with more appropriate coping strategies. Various group psychotherapies including play therapy, psychodrama and social-skills training may also be used. Behaviour therapy, on the other hand, attempts to change behaviour by unlearning undesirable and re-learning desirable behaviours.

Essentially, all the therapies (individual or group) can be traced back to three great intellectual traditions: the behavioural, psychoanalytic and humanistic models. The *behavioural* model – using behaviour therapy techniques such as fear reduction, assertiveness training, family therapy – assumes that maladaptive behaviour is learned and persists because of the individual's learning history and current interactions with the environment. Treatment is therefore an educational experience because just as maladaptive behaviour is learned it can be unlearned and replaced by new adaptive behaviours. The major focus of treatment is on the (measurable) change of some specific problem or source of distress. Behaviour therapists attempt to assess and modify a client's behaviour in the client's natural setting rather than in the consulting room or hospital. Behaviour treatments are adapted and tailored for each patient so that well-established procedures are moulded to each patient's particular needs. Finally, each treatment is an experiment in specifying objective goals and measuring progress during treatment.

The *psychoanalytic* and *psychodynamic* models cover a variety of approaches too diverse to find many points of consensus. They may be supportive, re-educative or reconstructive. Psychoanalysis – developed by Freud – aims to make a person aware of repressed impulses and for the person to recognize that these are the harmless residue of childhood fears and confusion. Patients are encouraged to free-associate by talking about whatever comes to mind, such as their early life, recent dreams, constant fears, problems at work. Occasionally the therapist offers some interpretation that must be perspicacious, properly timed and at the appropriate depth. The aim is insight into the origins and causes of specific problem behaviours which hopefully generalizes to the understanding of various new experiences, and to be aware of childhood sources of distress. The other psychodynamic therapies may differ according to which factors therapists feel are important (e.g. early childhood vs adolescence), the amount of emphasis they put on various motives (e.g. sex vs power, etc.). Nevertheless, they nearly all share the above attributes.

Finally, the *humanistic therapies* are pervasively optimistic, attempting to help people realize their potential. They are all concerned with the need for warm, close empathic interpersonal relationships and are very sensitive to depersonalization and alienation. Often this treatment is both non-directive and client-centred and the therapist attempts to be accurately empathic, non-possessively warm and genuine. The therapist does not assume the role of expert in making diagnostic interpretations but offers *unconditional positive regard*, (warmth, independent of behaviour) while attempting to stabilize the client's ideas. Existential psychotherapies tend to argue that "we are our choices" and that technique follows understanding. The encounter group (T-group, sensitivity group) movement is an outgrowth of the humanistic school.

Every treatment claims success but careful evaluative assessments tend to favour some treatments over others. For instance, behaviour therapy is particularly good at dealing with *phobias*, while psychodynamic theories are helpful in dealing with *guilt*.

Psychology at work: occupational psychology

How does one motivate workers? Are open-planned offices more efficient than old-fashioned "private" offices? What is the optimal organizational structure? For over eighty years psychologists have been intrigued by questions of behaviour at work, especially the problem of how to motivate workers.

About sixty years ago these questions were posed very simply. For instance, does the level of illumination in a factory or office affect worker productivity? In a now famous study carried out in a General Electric plant in Hawthorne, just outside Chicago, one group of females worked in a control room where the level of illumination was held constant; another group worked in a test room where brightness was varied up or down in a systematic manner. The results were rather odd: productivity increased in *both* the test and control rooms and there was no orderly relationship between level of illumination and productivity. The workers' output remained high in the test room even when illumination was reduced to that of moonlight. A researcher called in to interpret this finding then varied 13 different work-related factors and examined their effects on productivity. These included length of rest pauses, length of work day and work week, method of payment, place of work, the provision of a free lunch, etc. Again, female employees who worked in a special test room were used throughout the study. And again productivity increased with almost *every* change of work conditions and even when subjects were returned to the initial, standard conditions that existed at the start of the research, productivity continued to rise. These findings (commonly referred to as the "Hawthorne" effect) were replicated several times, with different tasks, different groups of workers and different settings. It was possible to demonstrate, however, that it was not only the *change* in working conditions that was responsible for the increased productivity.

The full answer turned out to be simple but nevertheless very important. The women in this factory knew that they were being observed and reacted very favourably to the special attention that they received and to the relatively free supervisory climate in that room. They said so when interviewed and were particularly sensitive to the warm human relationships on the shop-floor. It was the interest of the researchers rather than any of the numerous physical changes that caused the change in behaviour. This was to be the beginning of the human relations school which argued that the need for recognition, security and sense of belonging is more important in determining workers' morale and productivity than the physical conditions under which they work. Also, a complaint is not necessarily an objective recital of facts; it is often a symptom manifesting disturbance of an individual's status position. Further, the worker is a person whose attitudes and effectiveness are conditioned by social demands from both *inside* and *outside* the work plant. Similarly, informal groups within the work plant exercise strong social controls over the work habits and attitudes of the individual worker.

The question of motivation raises the difficult but interesting question of the relationship between job satisfaction and productivity. Three possible relationships occur: first, job satisfaction could cause (or lead to) productivity. Most people believe this to be true, namely that contented workers with high morale tend to work well. But this may be completely wrong. It is, for example, entirely possible that a *satisfied* worker could like his work and his fellow workers so well that his productivity would be adversely affected by frequent conversation. On the other hand, a *dissatisfied* worker might be extremely productive in order to progress to a more satisfying position or because of fear of his supervisor, losing his job, etc. Secondly, performance can lead to job satisfaction – high productivity leads to rewards which in turn lead to satisfaction. Where people are rewarded specifically for their effort and ability, they tend to be satisfied. However, where reward is not specifically related to performance level (i.e. a Christmas bonus for *all* employees) this is not likely to occur. Thirdly, of course there could be a situation where *both* or *neither* are true. In some cases satisfaction may cause productivity while in others productivity causes satisfaction *or* the two are unrelated. Group relations may have a very powerful effect which changes this relationship. For example, a satisfied worker may be influenced by his work group to restrict production if the organization does not respond with significant changes while a dissatisfied worker may be highly productive if the attitude of the work group is such that high performance is the accepted behaviour of the group as a whole.

Despite uncertainty about the relationship between satisfaction and productivity, employers have long attempted to motivate their employees to work harder – if possible to produce more and be more productive. A number of approaches have been tried, based on various theoretical traditions. *Need* theories suggest that people are motivated to satisfy various different needs which are hierarchically arranged. Thus, what an employer must do is create working conditions that satisfy basic needs (security, safety) so that employees can fully reach and exploit their potential. This approach has only been moderately successful. Another theoretical approach is based on the idea of social comparison and is called *equity* theory. It proposes that workers make comparisons between themselves and other workers with respect to what they get out of their job (outcomes) and what they contribute (input). Thus, if these are balanced one achieves equity; but if inputs exceed outputs one has underpayment inequity and resultant anger; and where outputs exceed inputs one has overpayment inequity and resultant guilt. The theory predicts that people strive to bring about equity – hence the self-perceived underpaid may work less hard and the overpaid more hard, but they may also achieve equity by simple rationalization, or theft or even resignation. A third theory, *expectancy/ valence* theory, has three basic factors that determine motivation: the expectancy that effort (work) will result in performance (productivity); the expectancy that performance will result in reward; that rewards are personally important and valuable. The theory suggests that employers should be careful: to determine what rewards (money, title, flexi-time) each employee values; to define the desired performance and what is expected; to make this desired performance possible and reasonably obtainable; and finally, to link these valued rewards to performance (Furnham 1992).

Perhaps the theory that has attracted most attention is the two-factor theory of motivation (Herzberg et al. 1959). The theory begins by challenging the assumption that job satisfaction and dissatisfaction are at opposite ends of the continuum. It suggests that the factors leading to satisfaction are different from those leading to dissatisfaction and thus should not be viewed as opposite ends of the same continuum. One group (dissatisfiers) cause a person to be *dissatisfied when not present* but are capable of causing *no satisfaction when present*. These include salary; working conditions; relationship with peers, subordinates and supervisors; and company policy and administration. Another set of factors (satisfiers) do not cause a person to be *dissatisfied when not present* but are the only elements capable of making him satisfied and motivated. These include opportunity for advancement, achievement, recognition and personal growth; responsibility and the intrinsic nature of the job itself.

One of the most popular ideas to emerge out of this theory was that of job enrichment by rotating and enlarging jobs. One does this in various steps by: *removing controls* from a job while retaining accountability; increasing the *accountability* of the individual for his own work; giving each person a *complete and natural module* of work; granting *job freedom* for a person's own work; making timely *reports on performance* available to the worker instead of to the supervisor; introducing *new tasks* not previously performed; assigning specific tasks so the employee can *develop expertise* in performing them. This has been done in a number of organizations. However, it is not always possible partly because technology often dictates job design but also because people resist it – managers because they fear loss of control, and employees because they fear change.

The above theory, along with all the others, has been challenged and in certain circumstances has been found wanting. These theories do not always work in all circumstances but if used judiciously in appropriate circumstances can be very effective. Certainly research has demonstrated that to motivate workers effectively managers should set clear, specific, difficult but obtainable goals and provide workers with feedback on how they are doing. Motivation can often be enhanced by organizational restructuring so that workers have more and more varied tasks at the same level and greater control over their jobs. If workers can experience meaningfulness at work (can identify with their task and see its significance); if they experience autonomy and resultant responsibility for the outcomes of the work; and if by feedback they gain knowledge of their actual performance, then results show workers are likely to experience higher internal motivation and satisfaction, a higher quality of work performance and lower absenteeism and turnover rates.

Psychology and the media

How effective are the television, radio and newspapers at manipulating the mind? Do television programmes about violence increase the likelihood that viewers will become violent? By contrast, do programmes showing pro-social, altruistic behaviour promote goodness? Does the portrayal of men and women in their traditional roles (i.e. doctors as men, nurses as women) perpetuate sex roles? One of the ways in which non-democratic governments (military dictatorships; one-party systems) attempt to prevent opposition and public debate is through strict control of the media and what it broadcasts. Does it work?

First, how pervasive is the influence of the media? Recent statistics have shown that (a) almost *every household* in the UK has at least one television set, (b) on average the set is *turned on* for almost six hours per day, (c) both *adults* and *children* watch more than *three hours* per day, (d) around *40 per cent* of all leisure time is devoted to television, (e) after sleep and work, television is the *greatest consumer of time*.

In the 1970s and 1980s 80 per cent of American television programmes and 90 per cent of children's-hour shows contained some violence. Between the ages of 5 and 15 a young viewer may witness the violent death of about 13,400 people on the screen. Various studies have been done – using different experimental techniques – to examine the effects of portraying anti-social behaviour on the television.

Many cases have been reported of people copying or imitating what they have seen on the television. One Los Angeles 7-year-old put ground glass in the family meal just as he had seen it done on the television. Within a few days after television programmes depicted a bank raid where robbers threatened to detonate bombs they had attached to themselves, five separate robberies of this sort were reported in Los Angeles despite the fact that no incident of this kind had ever been reported before. Some people might argue that these imitators are unbalanced criminals, small children or otherwise unlike ordinary people. But more careful investigations have shown a link between violent television and anti-social behaviour. In one study, groups of adolescent, male juvenile delinquents who were living in small group cottages were carefully observed for three weeks and their aggressive behaviour assessed (physical threats, verbal aggression, assaults, wanton destruction of inanimate objects). Then the boys in one cottage were exposed to five violent commercial films over a one-week period while boys in another cottage saw non-violent films. Those who had seen the violent movies showed a significant increase in most types of aggression over their original rate while the non-violent movie watchers did not.

In another study researchers found a positive association between 8-year-old children's preferences for violent television, radio and comic books and peer ratings of aggressiveness (correlation of .21). Ten years later, the same children were investigated to see if aggressive behaviour at age 18 could be predicted from knowledge of viewing habits in early childhood. There was a stronger positive correlation of .31 between preference for violent television programmes at 8 and aggression at 18 even when the effects of intelligence, socio-economic background and initial aggressiveness were controlled for. Many other studies have shown similar results.

In different countries, with different age groups, using different types of violent material, research demonstrates that television violence has definite effects on viewers. Some have argued the precise opposite, namely that watching violence gets it out of your system. This is the *vicarious catharsis hypothesis* that argues that seeing others' distress drains off one's own unhappiness or that reading pornography reduces the probability of sexual attacks. Various attempts have been made to test this theory. They usually involve getting two groups of people, angering one group (by insults, etc.) but not the other. Then half of each group (angered and non-angered) are shown violent television films while the other half of each group see non-violent films. After that, all the volunteers are given the opportunity to give electric shocks to the person who insulted them. Several studies have shown that regardless of how much anger was aroused, people who saw violent films deliver more shocks than subjects who saw non-violent films; that anger-aroused people respond more violently and that angered volunteers who witness aggression respond most aggressively of all. Thus there seems to be little support for the vicarious catharsis idea.

But can television promote helping, compassion, courtesy and affection by portraying pro-social behaviour? The answer is yes. One study looked at sports players (little league baseball, lacrosse and ice hockey). Players' pro-social behaviour (team work, caring for another's plight, displays of respect, apologizing) was measured before half were shown a pro-social control video. The level of pro-social behaviour increased following exposure to pro-social television for the hockey and lacrosse players but not the baseball players. Another study involved showing nearly a hundred 4-year-olds pro-social, aggressive and neutral films. The researchers then recorded the children's self-control by looking at their obedience to rules, persistence at tasks and tolerance at delaying gratification. Aggressive films decrease obedience and ability to tolerate delay while pro-social films increased obedience up to two weeks later. The effect of the pro-social films was to increase persistence at tasks on both immediate and later observation.

The same results apply to political messages and advertisements. Otherwise, why would American advertisers spend billions of dollars a year on television advertising if those repetitive brief exposures of their product did not modify the public's view of that product and lead them to buy more? People learn from television and what they learn depends on what they watch. The media in general is a source of observational learning experiences and a setter of norms. Television partly determines what we believe to be acceptable and appropriate behaviour in a variety of situations.

The media in general is a very powerful force in manipulating the mind.

Cognitive psychology: artificial intelligence

In the previous chapter we mentioned the burgeoning of cognitive psychology and its involvement with other disciplines such as anthropology, philosophy, neuroscience, linguistics and computer science to form the broader discipline of cognitive science. One of the most productive of these liaisons, particularly that between psychologists and computer scientists, has resulted in the study and application of artificial intelligence, or AI as it is more commonly known. Psychologists have been attracted to AI for a variety or reasons ranging from the simple acceptance that computers are powerful and useful tools in assisting in the development and testing of theories to the view that a properly programmed computer is literally a mind. This latter view is consistent with the belief in some quarters that people can be seen as information-processing systems, that mental activity consists of a series of computations and that mental processes are simply the manipulation of symbolic representations of the world (and ourselves) according to a series of rules. This view raises also the question of the relationship between mental events and physical processes. It is recognized that brains are not the same as computers in the hardware sense. The components of our brains are living nerve cells, neurones, whereas computers carry out their computations using inanimate materials, silicon chips and a variety of metals. Any similarities between brains and computers must lie in the software, that is in their information-processing routines, programs and memory stores. Most effort has gone into simulating the human processes of vision, speech perception, reasoning and decision making. The potential application of all of this work in industry, entertainment and medicine is enormous.

It has to be said, however, that progress so far has not quite caught up with the artificial intelligence portrayed in fiction by the robots R2D2 and C3PO in *Star Wars* or the computer HAL–9000 which features so prominently in the film *2001: A space odyssey*, based on a book by Arthur C. Clarke. At one point in Clarke's story, for instance, the stricken spaceship's captain David Bowman begins to disconnect one of HAL's memory units to correct a malfunction and as HAL realizes what is happening it says "Stop, Dave. I'm afraid, Dave. Dave, my mind is going; I can feel it." HAL appears not only to be able to think creatively but to experience emotions. So far computer systems do not, as far as we know, experience emotions but they can think creatively, learn from their mistakes and employ detours when their mental processes are blocked. The other thing which impresses us about HAL is that it can hold a conversation which it would be hard to distinguish from that of another human being. In fact the latter formed the basis of a test for the effectiveness of computer simulation of human performance suggested by Turing (1950) in the very early days of AI. If a person were allowed to interrogate both an "intelligent" computer system and a human being, could the interrogator tell from their answers alone which was which? One unintentional test of this sort is contained in the following (true) story about the vice president of a computer company in America who was hoping to demonstrate the system to a potential customer. Next to the computer's keyboard was a message which read "Type in all messages and end them with a full stop". The vice president assumed this was an invitation to contact his chief programmer via the computer's electronic mail system. In fact the keyboard was accessing a program which had been designed to produce responses similar to those which a non-directive psychotherapist might use with a patient. One of the "tricks" built in was the strategy of answering a question with another question . The following is the conversation which ensued over the keyboard between the vice president (VP) and the computer program (COMP) which displayed its response on the screen.

VP: Do you think that I can use the computer this morning?
COMP: Why do you ask?
VP: I think I might be able to make some additional sales.
COMP: Why aren't you sure?
VP: My prospective customers have never seen a demonstration of the system.
COMP: Does this mean very much to you?
VP: Of course it does.
COMP: You seem very positive about that.
VP: This is ridiculous.
COMP: What do you mean this is ridiculous?
VP: Is there any reason why I can't use the computer now?
COMP: Tell me more about your prospective customers.
VP: Please telephone me back on 491-1850

After this last input the VP forgot to end with a full stop and the computer therefore did not respond. The infuriated VP resorted to an earlier technology and telephoned his chief programmer (PROG) directly and shouted down the phone:

VP: Why are you being so snotty to me?
PROG: What do you mean why am I being snotty to you?

It apparently took some time for the programmer to calm the VP down.

Turing's test has since been criticized on a number of grounds. It is for example as much a test of the ingenuity of the person who is asking the questions as it is of the program itself. Also, even if the simulation is perfect there is no guarantee that the computer and the human brain are achieving their effect through the same type of information processing. The latter is of course very important for theory in AI though arguably less important in practice.

To take just one example of a development in AI which has had important applications, we could point to the modelling of decision-making processes which has led to *expert systems*. To solve problems both humans and computers need a good solid base of background information about the type of problem under consideration and some strategy for tackling the problem. The information base can be established through learning in humans and can be programmed into the computer. Generally speaking there are two major ways of tackling problems. One is to explore every possible solution in a strict logical order. Computers are very good at this, much quicker than humans. Even so it has been pointed out that a computer programmed to play chess solely on this basis would need to calculate so many possible sequences of moves to ensure victory on the greatest number of occasions that it would occupy much of the world's computer power for years (Solso 1979). What is needed are heuristics, the computational equivalent of human-like common sense "rules of thumb", which until recently computers have tended to lack. A heuristic might, for example, specify the most logical place to start looking for a solution to the problem or, in the case of the chess program, of eliminating all moves which place the most important pieces in immediate danger of being taken.

One of the early expert systems with some of these features is MYCIN which helps doctors to diagnose disease and to prescribe antibiotics (Shortliffe, 1976). MYCIN includes a knowledge base contributed by a number of (human) medical experts and an ability to ask the right sort of questions. MYCIN begins by reviewing the patient's symptoms and medical history and uses this information to identify the most likely cause of the symptoms. If MYCIN needs more information and cannot find it by searching its own information base, it requests the information from the doctor. MYCIN can then suggest a diagnosis and treatment giving the precise reasons for its decisions. Other expert systems are used in science, industry and business. As useful as expert systems like MYCIN are, they are still limited in that they are restricted to single areas of expertise, they are not generalists, they depend on knowledge fed to them by humans, and they can still from time to time show a striking lack of common sense when they persist with an answer which the human operator knows intuitively is wrong. Other systems such as SOAR (Newell 1990) are being developed to overcome these restrictions. SOAR has increased capabilities of learning from its own experience, can operate the equivalent of mental short-cuts once it has solved a similar problem before, and can explore mental detours when it reaches the sort of logical impasse which leads other programs to stop and generate an error message.

There is still a long way to go in the computer simulation of human mental processes. Computer programs do not yet enable the systems in which they sit to see, hear, understand or produce speech, experience emotions and have feelings in quite the way humans do, although some remarkable progress has been made towards this goal in some of these areas. It is fairly safe to predict that the products of cognitive science and AI research will change all of our lives in the coming years.

Psychologists everywhere

Attempts to understand and change behaviour are ubiquitous. Politicians and advertisers, health educators and pressure groups all devote a lot of effort to changing public opinions and behaviour. Nearly all of these groups are clearly not disinterested parties as they have a great deal to gain from achieving their objectives. However, there are many social science researchers (psychologists, sociologists, business administrators) who are involved in applied behavioural studies and do not directly gain from the successful "manipulation of the mind". Some are employed by government agencies and businesses to facilitate the change process. The application of psychological ideas to many areas of everyday life has greatly increased. To conclude this chapter we shall consider some of the more recent areas of application.

More and more psychological applications to *sport* have occurred in trying to help both professionals and non-professionals by providing them with information on how to maximize their performance while at the same time minimizing the harmful effects of competition and stress. Knowing how suitable a player's personality and mental health is to a particular sport is clearly important. Thus aggressiveness, masculinity and anxiety may be more appropriate in some sports than others. People who play individual sports (squash, boxing) may need to be more self-sufficient and self-centred while team sportsmen (baseball, volleyball) may need to be more dependable and reliable. The "fit" between the personality of the coach and the player is also relevant. The psychological and physical benefits of exercise are well known – exercise often reduces aggression, hypertension and excess weight while simultaneously improving self-confidence and emotional control. Watching sports – even on film – often leads to tension and aggression, and many countries in Europe and South America have witnessed spectator violence. Once again social scientists have provided useful advice on how to deal with this potential danger.

Psychology applied to all aspects of the world of *health* has also grown enormously in recent years. In the case of dentistry, for example, studies of dental attitudes, habits and knowledge, as well as fear of dentists, have enabled dentists to become much more effective in their treatment. For instance, it may be possible to distinguish the demographic profile of the preventive patient (who visits the dentist every six months as advised) and the restorative patient (who goes only when in pain). The former is more likely to be of a higher socio-economic class, with few fatalistic beliefs and low anxiety scores. He or she is also likely to have good oral hygiene practices and is discriminating about the type of dentist and dental treatment he or she chooses. The restorative patient, who goes only when in trouble, is likely to be of a lower socio-economic class, highly anxious, fatalistic and with poor dental habits and knowledge yet curiously trusting in the dentist. Fear of dentists and fear of pain are major concerns and there are now many ways to treat them such as modelling (watching others) and systematic desensitization (gradual approaches to the stressful situation while being relaxed). Bruxism, the tendency to grind one's teeth, is also a topic of interest in behavioural dentistry as its causes (and cures) are psychological.

Psychology is now well on the way to making important contributions to *traffic safety*. The visibility and legibility of road signs has been an important topic of research – the size, shape and colour of words on different backgrounds makes them more, or less, readable. The ergonomics (anthropometry) of seating design and panel displays is also important to maximize safety and comfort. Pedals, knobs, levers, switches, dials, clocks, counters must all be designed for effectiveness. Most important, however, is the work which sets out to understand and manipulate the mind of the driver. What sort of people are more likely to cause accidents? Highly prone groups include the anxious, aggressive, impulsive, socially maladjusted, dependent, egocentric, tense and those intolerant of stress. Various drugs like tranquillizers, antihistamines, pep pills and especially alcohol are capable of affecting alertness, reaction times and general perceptual motor co-ordination which in turn increases the likelihood of accidents. In fact, it was psychologists who invented the breathalyser and advised on the maximum legal limit of alcohol permissible in the blood stream for safe driving. This was only done after years of careful experiments testing people in various stages of intoxication on simulated driving tasks.

Psychologists work in the *military* – in all branches and at all levels. They advise about reducing military stress and how stress leads to poor decision making. They are also involved in selection and promotion. It costs well over one million pounds to fully train a fighter pilot whose aircraft may cost up to anything as much as ten million pounds. One small miscalculation, lack of attention or irrational fear response could cause a crash leading to the death of the pilot and the destruction of the machine. Hence it is essential that pilots are selected for their physiological as well as psychological suitability to a difficult and stressful job. Similarly, extensive historical and simulated studies on military incompetence reveal how, why and when commanders make serious and crucial errors of judgement.

It is not only the mind of man that social scientists have attempted to manipulate. Psychologists with a particular interest in *animals* have applied behaviour therapy techniques with neurotic animals in zoos, in vets' surgeries or in people's homes and have looked at the psychological effects pets have on their owners. Psychologists may also be found on farms, attempting for example to establish under what conditions animals are best looked after to produce more milk or bigger eggs.

Psychologists work in prisons, in educational establishments, in old-age homes and for television companies; they research on everything from electricity consumption to fear of flying. Many are interested in changing people's ideas, attitudes, knowledge and behaviour, usually but not always for people's own benefit. More and more useful techniques are being found to manipulate the mind. There are examples of research which could be applied, but which has not been, and of wrongly applied research. But by and large the research of applied academic psychologists has been put to good use attempting to promote general human welfare.

There are those who are concerned not so much by the uses as the abuses of psychology. Certainly psychiatrists and no doubt some psychologists have been used by repressive governments to attempt to help them to control dissidents of various kinds. Psychology is as useful in warfare as welfare. How and when it is applied is a social-policy question. But psychologists are deeply concerned with ethical issues and are often honour-bound by learned and professional societies to follow strict codes of conduct.

It is the diversity of human behaviours and problems that is the major cause of the variety of topics in psychology. We have only been able to provide a brief glimpse here of the many, varied and different activities of professional and academic psychologists. We haven't even touched on the role of *environmental* and *educational* psychology. But to get a full list of the areas of concern to psychologists, take a look at the next chapter.

Chapter 6
Taking things further

Our intention has been to give you a flavour of psychology, and to convey some of the excitement of this new and constantly developing discipline in order that you may decide whether it is something you wish to pursue further. You could, if you wished, read more about the subject yourself or study psychology more formally at school, college or university simply for interest – and we believe that most of you would not be disappointed in that. This would be true whether your current inclination lies in the arts and humanities or in the sciences. Especially perhaps if you are unable to decide between the two. Psychology can give you the best of both worlds. Aside from interest you may be thinking of a career, or perhaps a change in career. In that case you may wish to obtain a university degree in psychology to use as a general, all-round qualification to enter industry or commerce or perhaps you will decide to go on to become a professional psychologist yourself. So, whatever your goals, and if your appetite has been whetted by what you have read so far, where do you go from here?

This chapter is intended as a brief guide to further your exploration of psychology. It refers primarily to the British system because that is the one we know best. However, psychology both as an academic discipline and as a professional activity is an international enterprise and does not differ substantially in America, Africa, Australia, New Zealand, Hong Kong or wherever it is studied. This is particularly the case where English is the language used for teaching as so many of the textbooks are produced in the UK and in America for worldwide markets. We hope you will find what follows useful and relevant wherever you intend to study, although some of the information and the details of the educational system may not apply specifically to you. In general, schools, careers offices, public libraries, academic bookshops and careers counsellors are good sources of local information, as are past and present students of psychology. We have given the addresses of some national psychological societies at the end of this chapter.

Reading more about psychology

As we said at the end of Chapter 4, you could follow up some of the references we have given you to specific studies in the course of this book, but first we would recommend that you look at one of the many general textbooks in psychology. These give a much more detailed picture of the subject and in particular of the content of academic courses in psychology. There are a great many texts to choose from and the following is a selection of those which we have found most useful.

School and college textbooks (GCSE and A/AS level)

Hayes, N. 1993. *A first course in psychology*, 3rd edn. Walton on Thames, Surrey: Nelson.

Hayes, N. & S. Orrell 1993. *Psychology: an introduction*, 2nd edn. Harlow, Essex: Longman.

General textbooks originating in the UK (A/AS level and first-year degree level)

Gross, R. D. 1992. *Psychology: the science of mind and behaviour*, 2nd edn. London: Hodder & Stoughton.

Hayes, N. 1994. *Foundations of psychology: an introductory text*. London & New York: Routledge.

Radford, J. & E. T. Govier (eds) 1991. *A textbook of psychology*, 2nd edn. London & New York: Routledge.

General textbooks originating in the USA (up to and including first-year degree level)

Atkinson, R. L., R. C. Atkinson, E. E. Smith, D. J. Bem 1993. *Introduction to psychology*, 11th edn. New York & London: Harcourt Brace Jovanovich.

Gleitman, H. 1991. *Psychology*, 3rd edn. New York & London: Norton.

Goldstein, E.B. 1994. *Psychology*. Pacific Grove, California: Brooks/Cole.

Huffman, K., M. Vernoy, J. Vernoy 1994. *Psychology in action*, 3rd edn. New York: Wiley.

Kalat, J. W. 1993. *Introduction to psychology*, 3rd edn. Pacific Grove, California: Brooks/Cole.

Learning more about psychology

Psychology can be studied for general interest through courses offered at adult education centres and university extra-mural departments. They are usually open to anyone with an interest in the subject but do not normally lead to any recognized qualification. It is also possible to study psychology (at GCSE, A and AS level) in schools and colleges. The GCSE course provides a simple introduction to the main areas of psychology and covers topics such as play, attitudes, prejudice, intelligence, personality, perception and language. The A level takes things a little further, looking at theories and methods, and allows students the opportunity to do some practical work of their own. Areas covered may include abnormal psychology, memory, child development, animal behaviour and interpersonal attraction. The AS level is equivalent to half an A level, covering many of the same areas and again allowing for some practical involvement in the subject via project work. Universities and some colleges offer first-degree courses (BSc and BA) in psychology, usually lasting for three years and covering the whole of psychology. To enter one of these courses, unless you are a mature student, it is usually necessary to have three A-level subjects (or equivalent Scottish or international qualifications) at good grades. Two AS levels may be offered in place of an A level. There are usually no specified subjects required at A or AS level but most psychology departments will ask for GCSE mathematics, usually at grade C or better (to ensure that you can cope with the statistics part of the course). As well as numeracy, psychology courses require literacy and a willingness to adopt scientific methodology. A good preparation for a degree in psychology might therefore include the following school subjects (A or AS level): (a) biology or human biology, (b) mathematics and (c) one of English, history, economics or other arts/humanities subject where psychology can be seen to be relevant. Having said that, it is also true that psychology departments like their students to be as diverse in their interests as the subject they wish to study and applicants are accepted who are offering all arts/humanities subjects or all science subjects as well as those with a mixture of the two at A level. Increasing numbers of students are entering university psychology courses having already studied A- or AS-level psychology but it is probably fair to say that most departments do not discriminate either for or against students who have this prior exposure to the subject. They all teach on the assumption that students will have no knowledge of psychology. There is one advantage to having taken psychology prior to university entry and that is that it gives the prospective student a chance to find out what the subject is really about and also to decide whether they want to take it further. The disadvantage is that it restricts the range of experience of other disciplines which the prospective student can bring to their study of psychology at the higher level. The most important consideration, however, is that students should take those school subjects (A and AS level) they have an interest in. Psychology is a very competitive area and good A- or AS-level grades (or their equivalents) are important.

Before applying for a degree course it is important to research what is on offer by reading university prospectuses and psychology department booklets, talking to careers advisers and former students and going to one or more of the many open days. One issue which may arise is whether to take a single-degree course in psychology or joint honours, where a second subject is studied alongside psychology. If you are committed to the possibility of a career in psychology a single-degree course is the most appropriate. Otherwise, you may wish to opt for a broader educational background albeit at the cost of having to keep up with the academic workload in two subject areas rather than just one. If you are considering a career in school teaching, a joint degree where the other subject is one which is currently part of the National Curriculum may be an advantage. If you choose either a single or joint degree and you think you may wish to go on to further training and professional work in psychology you should check with the particular psychology department you are interested in that the course on offer meets the requirements for graduate membership of the British Psychological Society and the graduate basis for registration as a chartered psychologist. Another consideration is your age. Mature students are subject to individual, and flexible admission criteria. The normal three A-level requirement discussed above does not apply. If you will be 21 years of age or older in the proposed year of entry and wish to apply to a university or college as a higher-degree student, it is worth writing to the departmental admissions tutor for advice on your particular case. It also is perhaps worth noting that most psychology departments actively welcome applications from mature students for the practical experience of life which they can bring to their studies.

The sources listed below will help to get you started on your information search.

- All applications for university and college degree courses are dealt with through UCAS (Universities and Colleges Admissions Service). Schools and colleges will usually provide their students with the appropriate booklets and application forms for entry to degree courses. If you are not currently studying, or in case of difficulty, write to: UCAS, PO Box 28, Cheltenham, Gloucestershire GL50 3SA.
- The most authoritative guide to all of the university degrees in the UK, the entry requirements, the addresses to write to for individual prospectuses and departmental booklets as well as information about each of the universities is: *University and college entrance: official guide*. This is published annually by UCAS and is available from bookshops or libraries, or by writing to: Sheed & Ward, 14 Coopers Row, London EC3N 2BH.
- Publications more specifically featuring psychology degrees are: A. Gale, *Which psychology degree course?* (1993). This helpful paperback, as well as a free leaflet "Studying Psychology", is published

by the British Psychological Society. Both are obtainable from them at the address given at the end of this chapter. Also CRAC *degree course guide: psychology*. This very reasonably priced booklet published by Hobsons on behalf of the Careers Research Advisory Centre is one of a range of subject-area guides. It is updated every two years and is obtainable by writing to: Client Services Department, Biblios Publishers' Distribution Service Ltd, Star Road, Partridge Green, West Sussex RH13 8LD.

Using a psychology degree: thinking of careers in psychology

As we have said, psychology is a broadly based subject requiring of its practitioners numeracy, literacy (written and oral communication skills) and an appreciation of research methods. Most psychology degrees also foster good interpersonal skills, computer literacy and an ability to think independently. These are abilities which employers are looking for in a wide range of careers and occupations, and it is perhaps not too surprising that many psychology graduates find employment in areas outside the mainstream of professional psychology. In fact it has been estimated that only 25 per cent of psychology graduates go on to become professional psychologists. The remainder compete very effectively with other graduates and choose to enter the public service (such as the civil service, armed forces and the National Health Service), computer science, education, industry, commerce (such as banking, accounting, insurance) and other professions (such as advertising, publishing, personnel management, entertainment, journalism and law). Even so, most of these graduates find some of what they have learned in their psychology course relevant to their adopted careers and to their promotion prospects. Indeed, there are very few areas of human activity where a knowledge of psychology is not helpful. Nevertheless, even in some clearly related careers the graduate will need to obtain further specialist qualifications – examples are social work, occupational therapy, physiotherapy, art therapy, counselling and nursing.

Those who do go on to become professional psychologists may enter careers in pure or applied research or in teaching at a variety of levels. Others enter the more applied professional areas, a number of which were mentioned in Chapter 5. For some of these, and in particular clinical psychology, occupational psychology, criminological and legal psychology, and educational psychology, a further degree course (at masters or doctoral level) or special examination is required plus a period of relevant practical experience. In some cases this can add up to four or five more years before the full professional qualification is obtained.

There are no very precise data on the proportion of individuals which these various career destinations involve. But there are some indications. A recent analysis of what psychology students in the UK do immediately after graduating, for example, indicates that 58% go directly into permanent employment (this includes some who are gaining experience before going on to professional training courses in psychology), 15% go on to do research or academic study, 12% take up teacher training, 12% enter directly into other training and 8% take on short-term employment of various sorts. In terms of the types of full-time employment which psychologists take up, 39% enter the public service, 6% go into education, 12% into industry, 26% into commerce and 17% find themselves in other forms of employment too varied to categorize more precisely.

The following inexpensive publications give a good overview of the careers entered by psychology graduates and have lists of sources for more detailed information. These and a free leaflet "Opportunities and careers for psychologists" are obtainable from the British Psychological Society (address at the end of this chapter): L. T. Higgins, *How about psychology? A guide to courses and careers* (1986); S. Newstead, *Putting psychology to work* (1989) and L. T. Higgins, *Career choices in psychology* (1991).

Table 6.1 is based on the British Psychological Society's list of services offered by chartered psychologists and whilst it is not totally comprehensive, it does give a good overview of the areas in which professional psychologists work. A chartered psychologist is someone who (i) has successfully completed a first qualification in psychology, (ii) has undergone a further period of supervised training in a specific area of psychology and (iii) has been judged to be fit to practise psychology without supervision. In addition, to appear on the Register of Chartered Psychologists the individual must agree to abide by the British Psychological Society's Code of Conduct, which is backed up by a disciplinary system administered by a panel consisting of a majority of non-psychologists. The Register of Chartered Psychologists and the associated Directory of Chartered Psychologists is a means whereby members of the general public can identify fully trained psychologists answerable to a professional regulatory body and so protect themselves from self-styled practitioners who profess to offer psychological services. The Directory of Chartered Psychologists is published by the British Psychological Society, whose address is at the end of this chapter.

The corresponding society representing the interests of professional psychologists in America is the American Psychological Association. Table 6.2 is a list of divisions of the American Psychological Association. It is a list of "interests" rather than professional services offered. Taken in conjunction with Table 6.1, it helps to fill out the picture of how professional psychologists see themselves and the work they do.

Table 6.1 Areas in which chartered psychologists offer services (1994).

1.0 *Clinical psychology services*
1.1 Adult mental health – general
1.2 Adult mental health – rehabilitation
1.3 Child clinical psychology
1.4 Learning disabilities (mental handicap)
1.5 Elderly people
1.6 Health psychology (including HIV/AIDS)
1.7 Neuropsychology
1.8 Addictive behaviours
1.9 Forensic services
1.10 Sensory and physical disabilities
1.11 Research
1.12 Teaching
1.13 Management and planning
2.0 *Clinical neuropsychology services*
2.1 Head injury (adults)
2.2 Neurological disease (adults)
2.3 Childhood disorders (developmental and acquired)
2.4 Congenital disorders
2.5 Disorders of the elderly
2.6 Medico-legal services
2.7 Behavioural disorders
3.0 *Counselling psychology services*
3.1 Adults
3.2 Students and young people
3.3 Families and couples
3.4 Elderly
3.5 Health/medical
3.6 Group work
3.7 Organizational
3.8 Community/social
4.0 *Educational psychology services*
4.1 Adolescent counselling
4.2 Adults
4.3 Consultancy
4.4 Counselling
4.5 Disability and handicap
4.6 Dyslexia and specific learning difficulties
4.7 Family-focused work
4.8 Group work
4.9 Individual assessment
4.10 Individual therapy
4.11 Inservice training
4.12 Management of behaviour problems
4.13 Education Act
4.14 Organizational work
4.15 Pre-school work
4.16 Research and evaluation

5.0 *Criminological and legal services*
5.1 The assessment of offenders
5.2 The management of individuals prior to sentencing
5.3 The management of offenders following sentencing
5.4 The victims of crime
5.5 Family/domestic issues and children
5.6 Policy issues
6.0 *Occupational psychology services*
6.1 Counselling and personal development
6.2 Design of environments and of work
6.3 Employee relations and motivation
6.4 Human–machine interaction
6.5 Organizational development
6.6 Performance appraisal and career development
6.7 Personnel selection and assessment
6.8 Training
7.0 *Psychological services in social services settings*
7.1 Adoption and fostering
7.2 Care of the elderly in the community
7.3 Child protection
7.4 Counseling and direct psychological interventions with clients
7.5 Ethnicity issues
7.6 Gender issues
7.7 Implications of legislation
7.8 Managerial advice
7.9 Personnel selection
7.10 Psychological aspects of disasters
7.11 Services to people with learning disabilities
7.12 Teaching psychological skills and counselling
8.0 *Services by teachers of psychology*
8.1 Assessment
8.2 Curriculum
8.3 Educational resources
8.4 Skill-based education
8.5 Teaching style
9.0 *Other psychological services*
9.1 Health psychology
9.2 Sports psychology
9.3 Market, social and consumer research
9.4 Psychological research

Table 6.2. Divisions of the American Psychological Association (1994).

General psychology
Teaching of psychology
Experimental psychology
Evaluation, measurement and statistics
Physiological and comparative psychology
Developmental psychology
Society for Personality and Social Psychology
Society for the Study of Social Issues
Psychology and the arts
Clinical psychology
Consulting psychology
Society for Industrial and Organizational Psychology
Educational psychology
School psychology
Counseling psychology
Psychologists in public service
Military psychology
Adult development and aging
Applied experimental and engineering psychology
Rehabilitation psychology
Society for Consumer Psychology
Theoretical and philosophical psychology
Experimental analysis of behavior
History of psychology
Society for Commnity Research and Action
Psychopharmacology and substance abuse
Psychotherapy
Psychological hypnosis
State Psychological Association affairs
Humanistic psychology
Mental retardation and developmental disabilities
Population and environmental psychology
Psychology of women
Psychology of religion
Child, youth and family services
Health psychology
Psychoanalysis
Clinical neuropsychology
American Psychology – Law Society
Psychologists in independent practice
Family psychology
Society for the Psychological Study of Lesbian and Gay Issues
Society for the Psychological Study of Ethnic Minority Issues
Media psychology
Exercise and sport psychology
Peace psychology
Group psychology and group psychotherapy
Psychology of addictive behaviors

Conclusion

Why psychology? We hope that this book has provided at least some answers to that question and has helped you to decide whether you wish to know more. Inevitably there will be some areas which you will enjoy more than others but we believe psychology at some level has something for just about everyone. Certainly, psychology has retained our interest over a great many years and we hope some of our enthusiasm for our subject has been evident in these pages. Psychology is developing rapidly. It is about people and their activities, and people are the most fascinating subjects to study. To adapt a famous quotation: "To be tired of psychology is to be tired of life". We would not expect you to take our word for it of course. As professional psychologists we might be hopelessly biased on the subject. But if your curiosity has been aroused, do take the next step and follow up some of the sources of further information included in this chapter.

Some useful addresses

The British Psychological Society
St Andrews House
48 Princess Road East
Leicester LE1 7DR
UK

The British Psychological Society will send their publications overseas at a slightly higher rate to cover the cost of airmail postage. If you are living outside the UK, write to them in the first instance at the above address requesting a list of publications, prices and mailing charges. Credit card orders and orders from non-members of BPS can be placed with the distributors for BPS publications: Plymbridge Distributors Ltd, Estover, Plymouth PL6 7PZ, UK. (Tel: 0752 695745).

Other potential sources of information are:

American Psychological Association
750 First Street, NE
Washington DC
20002–4242
USA

Australian Psychological Society
1 Grattan Street
Carlton
Victoria 3053
Australia

National Research Council of Canada
c/o Dr A. Albagli
Head/International Affairs
Chemin de Montreal
Ottawa
Ontario K1S OR6
Canada

Société Française de Psychologie
28–32, rue Serpente
F–75006 Paris
France

Hong Kong Psychological Society Ltd
Department of Psychology
University of Hong Kong
Hong Kong

New Zealand Psychological Society
PO Box 4092
Wellington
New Zealand

Psychological Association of South
  Africa
c/o South African ICSU Secretariat
PO Box 395
Pretoria 0001
South Africa

References

Asch, S. E. 1956. Studies of independence and conformity: 1. A minority of one against a unanimous majority. *Psychological Monographs* **70** (whole no. 416).

Atkinson, R. L., R. C. Atkinson, E. E. Smith, D. J. Bem 1993. *Introduction to psychology*, 11th edn. New York & London: Harcourt Brace Jovanovich.

Baron-Cohen, S., A. M. Leslie, U. Frith 1985. Does the autistic child have a "theory of mind"? *Cognition* **21**, 37–46.

Bartlett, F. C. 1932. *Remembering: a study in experimental and social psychology*. Cambridge: Cambridge University Press.

Beyerstein, B. & D. Beyerstein (eds) 1992. *The write stuff: evaluations of graphology*. New York: Prometheus.

Bliss, E. L. 1986. *Multiple personality, allied disorders and hypnosis*. Oxford: Oxford University Press.

Bonke, B., P. I. M. Schmitz, F. Verhage, A. Zwaveling 1986. Clinical study of so-called unconscious perception during general anaesthesia. *British Journal of Anaesthesiology* **14**, 957–64.

Brandsma, J. M. & A. M. Ludwig 1974. A case of multiple personality: diagnosis and therapy. *International Journal of Clinical and Experimental Hypnosis* **22**, 216–33.

Brion, S. & C. P. Jedynak 1972. Troubles du transfer inter hémispherique: le signe de la main étrangère. *Revue Neurologique* **126**, 257–66.

Cheek, D. B. & L. M. Le Cron 1968. *Clinical hypnotherapy*. New York: Grune & Stratton.

Chertok, L. 1981. *Sense and nonsense in psychotherapy: the challenge of hypnosis*. Oxford: Pergamon Press.

Colman, A. 1988. *What is psychology? The inside story*. London: Hutchinson.

Conklin, E. 1919. Superstitious beliefs and practice among college students. *American Journal of Psychology* **30**, 83–102.

Dimond, S. J. 1979. Symmetry and asymmetry in the vertebrate brain. In *Brain, behaviour and evolution*, D. A. Oakley & H. C. Plotkin (eds), 139–59. London: Methuen.

Eagly, A. H. & C. Chrvala 1986. Sex differences in conformity: status and gender-role interpretations. *Psychology of Women Quarterly* **10**, 203–20.

Eibl-Eibesfeldt, I. 1971. *Love and hate*. London: Methuen.

REFERENCES

Eysenck, H. 1957. *Sense and nonsense in psychology*. Harmondsworth: Penguin.

Festinger, L. & J. Carlsmith 1959. Cognitive consequences of forced compliance. *Journal of Abnormal and Social Psychology* **58**, 203–10.

Fletcher, C., D. Rose & J. Radford 1991. Employers' perceptions of psychology graduates. *The Psychologist* **4**, 434–39.

Freud, S. 1901. *The psychopathology of everyday life*, repr. 1960. New York: Norton.

Freud, S. 1910. *Leonardo da Vinci: a study in psychosexuality*, repr. 1947. New York: Random House.

Furnham, A. 1992. *Personality at work*. London: Routledge.

Gale, A. 1993. *Which psychology degree course?* Leicester: British Psychological Society.

Garcia, J. & R. A. Koelling 1966. Relation of cue to consequence in avoidance learning. *Psychonomic Science* **4**, 123–4.

Gazzaniga, M. S., J. E. Le Doux, D. H. Wilson 1977. Language, praxis, and the right hemisphere: some clues to mechanisms of consciousness. *Neurology* **24**, 1144–7.

Gleitman, H. 1991. *Psychology*, 3rd edn. New York & London: Norton.

Goldstein, E. B. 1994. *Psychology*. Pacific Grove, Cal.: Brooks/Cole.

Gregory, C. 1975. Changes in superstitions and beliefs among college women. *Psychological Reports* **37**, 939–44.

Gross, R. D. 1992. *Psychology: the science of mind and behaviour*, 2nd edn. London: Hodder & Stoughton.

Gunter, B. 1987. *Poor reception: misunderstanding and forgetting broadcast news*. New York: Erlbaum.

Haney, C., C. Banks, P. Zimbardo 1978. Interpersonal dynamics in a simulated prison. *International Journal of Criminology and Penology* **1**, 69–97.

Happé, F. 1994. *Autism*. London: UCL Press.

Hayes. N. 1993. *A first course in psychology*, 3rd edn. Walton on Thames, Surrey: Nelson.

Hayes. N. 1994. *Foundations of psychology: an introductory text*. London & New York: Routledge.

Hayes, N. & S. Orrell 1993. *Psychology: an introduction*, 2nd edn. Harlow, Essex: Longman.

Herzberg, F., B. Mausner, B. Snyderman 1959. *The motivation to work*. New York: Wiley.

Hess, E. H. 1975. The role of pupil size in communication. *Scientific American* **233**, 110–19.

Higgins, L. T. 1986. *How about psychology? A guide to courses and careers*. Leicester: British Psychological Society.

Higgins, L. T. 1991. *Career choices in psychology*. Leicester: British Psychological Society.

Hilgard, E. R. 1977. *Divided consciousness: multiple controls in human thought and action*. London: John Wiley & Sons.

Huffman, K., M. Vernoy, J. Vernoy 1994. *Psychology in action*, 3rd edn. New York: Wiley.

Huxley, T. 1902. *Collected essays*. London: Methuen.

Insko, C. A., R. H. Smith, M. D. Alicke, J. Wade, S.Taylor 1985. Conformity and group size: the concern with being right and the concern with being liked.

Personality and Social psychology Bulletin **11**, 41–50.

Janet, P. 1889. *L'automatisme psychologique*. Paris: Felix Alcan.

Kalat, J. W. 1993. *Introduction to psychology*, 3rd edn. Pacific Grove, Cal.: Brooks/Cole.

Kaplan, E. A. 1960. Hypnosis and pain. *Archives of General Psychiatry* **2**, 567–8.

Levinson, B. W. 1965. States of awareness under general anaesthesia. *British Journal of Anaesthesiology* **37**, 544–6.

Levitt, E. 1952. Superstitions: twenty-five years ago and today. *American Journal of Psychology* **65**, 443–9.

Loftus, E. R. 1992. The reality of repressed memories. *American Psychologist* **48**, 518–37

Lundin, R. 1985. *Theories and systems of psychology*. Lexington: D. C. Heath.

McKeachie, W. & C. Doyle 1966. *Psychology*. Reading, Mass.: Addison-Wesley.

Milgram, S. 1963. Behavioural study of obedience. *Journal of Abnormal and Social Psychology* **67**, 371–8.

Morris, C. 1978. *Psychology: an introduction*. New Jersey: Prentice Hall.

Nachmias, C. & D. Nachmias 1981. *Research Methods in the Social Sciences*. London: Edward Arnold.

Neisser, U. & N. Harsch 1992. Phantom flashbulbs: false recollections of hearing the news about Challenger. In *Affect and accuracy in recall: studies of "flashbulb" memories*, E. Winograd & U. Neisser (eds), 9–31. New York: Cambridge University Press.

Newell, A. 1990. *Unified theories of cognition*. Cambridge, Mass.: Harvard University Press.

Newstead, S. 1989. *Putting psychology to work*. Leicester: British Psychological Society.

Nixon, H. 1925. Popular answers to some psychological questions. *American Journal of Psychology* **36**, 418–23.

Pavlov, I. P. 1927. *Conditioned reflexes*. New York: Oxford University Press.

Piaget, J. 1962. *Plays, dreams and imitation in childhood*. New York: Norton.

Porter, R. H. & J. D. Moore 1981. Human kin recognition by olfactory cues. *Physiology and Behavior* **27**, 493–5.

Radford, J. & E. T. Govier (eds) 1991. *A textbook of psychology*, 2nd edn. London & New York: Routledge.

Rosnow, R. & R. Rosenthal 1992. *Beginning behavioural research*. New York: Macmillan.

Sackheim, H. A., R. C. Gur, M. Saucy 1978. Emotions are expressed more intensely on the left side of the face. *Science* **202**, 434–6.

Schreiber, F. R. 1973. *Sybil*. Harmondsworth: Penguin.

Seligman, M. E. P. 1972. The sauce béarnaise phenomenon. In *Biological boundaries of learning*, Seligman, M. E. P. & J. L. Hager (eds), 8–9. New York: Appleton-Century-Crofts.

Shortliffe, E. H. 1976. Computer-based medical consultations, MYCIN. New York: Elsevier.

Skinner, B. F. 1938. *The behavior of organisms*. New York: Appleton-Century-Crofts.

Skinner, B. F. 1972. *Beyond freedom and dignity*. London: Jonathan Cape.

Smith, E. 1961. The power of dissonance techniques to change attitudes. *Public Opinion Quarterly* **25**, 626–39.

REFERENCES

Solso, R. L. 1979. *Cognitive psychology*. New York: Harcourt Brace Jovanovich.

Sperry, R. W. 1968. Hemisphere deconnection and unity in conscious awareness. *American Psychologist* **23**, 723–32,

Springer, S. P. & G. Deutsch 1989. *Left brain, right brain*, 3rd edn. New York: Freeman.

Tupper, V. & R. Williams 1986. Unsubstantiated beliefs among beginning psychology students. *Psychological Reports* **58**, 383–8.

Turing, A. M. 1950. Computing machinery and intelligence. *Mind* **59**, 433–60.

Watson, J. B. & R. Rayner 1920. Conditioned emotional reactions. *Journal of Experimental Psychology* **3**, 1–14.

Wilkie, W. 1990. *Consumer behavior*. New York: Wiley.

Wrightsman, L. 1964. Measurement of philosophies of human nature. *Psychological Reports* **14**, 743–51.

Index

INDEX